64 Things You Need to Know in Chess

John Walker

First published in the UK by Gambit Publications Ltd 2002

ISBN 1 901983 67 6

DISTRIBUTION:
Worldwide (except USA): Central Books Ltd, 99 Wallis Rd, London E9 5LN.
Tel +44 (0)20 8986 4854 Fax +44 (0)20 8533 5821. E-mail: orders@Centralbooks.com
USA: BHB International, Inc., 41 Monroe Turnpike, Trumbull, CT 06611, USA.

For all other enquiries (including a full list of all Gambit Chess titles) please contact the publishers, Gambit Publications Ltd, P.O. Box 32640, London W14 0JN.
E-mail Murray@gambitchess.freeserve.co.uk
Or visit the GAMBIT web site at http://www.gambitbooks.com

Edited by Graham Burgess
Typeset by Petra Nunn
Printed in Great Britain by The Cromwell Press, Trowbridge, Wilts.

10 9 8 7 6 5 4 3 2 1

Gambit Publications Ltd
Managing Director: GM Murray Chandler
Chess Director: GM John Nunn
Editorial Director: FM Graham Burgess
German Editor: WFM Petra Nunn

Contents

Symbols and Notation

Throughout this book we use the short form of algebraic notation.

The Board

Each row of squares across the board is called a *rank*, and is given a number starting from White's side.

Each row of squares running up the board is called a *file*, and is given a letter starting from White's left-hand side.

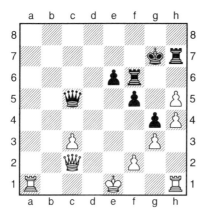

Each square is named by first giving the file letter and then the rank number. In our diagram a white rook stands on a1, the white queen at c2, the black king at g7 and so on.

The Symbols

We use symbols as abbreviations for pieces and some chess terms.

♔	King
♕	Queen
♖	Rook
♗	Bishop
♘	Knight

The pawn symbol is not used in chess notation.

0-0	castles on the kingside
0-0-0	castles on the queenside
x	takes
+	check
++	double check
#	checkmate
(D)	see next diagram

We use ! to show a good move and ? to show a bad move.

!! shows a move which is brilliant and very strong whilst ?? shows a terrible move.

Writing the Moves

There are five things that may be written when writing a move:

a) the symbol for the piece which moves (unless it is a pawn, in which case no symbol is used).

b) any necessary clarification of the file or rank from which the piece moves.

c) a capture sign, if a capture is being made.

d) the square to which the piece moves.

e) a check symbol if the move played gives check.

In the diagram in the previous column, the white rook that stands on a1 can move to a8. This would be written ♖**a8**.

If the black rook on h7 moved to h6, this would be written **...♖hh6**, to distinguish it from a move by the other rook from f6 to h6. The three dots signify that this is a move by Black.

If check is given, the check symbol will be written after the move. In the diagram White can give check with his rook on a7. This would be written ♖**a7+**.

But if White does give check with his rook Black could capture the rook with his queen. This would be written **...♛xa7**.

As the pawn has no symbol, the first of our five steps is left out when we write a pawn move. If White advances the pawn in front of his queen, the move is written simply as **c4**. When a pawn makes a capture, the file of departure is also given. Thus if White moved his f-pawn forward and Black then captured it, Black's move would be written as **...gxf3**.

Naming Pawns

A pawn is named according to the file on which it stands. In the diagram the pawn on c3 is White's c-pawn. The pawn on e6 is Black's e-pawn and so on.

Naming Pieces

If in the commentary it is necessary to distinguish between two similar pieces of the same colour, each is named according to the square it stands upon. In the diagram Black has two rooks, his f6-rook and his h7-rook.

Some Chess Terms and Expressions

Blunder: a very bad mistake.

Combination: a series of moves, generally including a sacrifice, aimed at gaining an advantage.

Centre: the middle of the board, in particular the squares d4, e4, d5 and e5.

En Prise: a piece is said to be *en prise* when it is attacked and its capture would result in a loss of material.

Exchange, the: the material advantage of a rook against a knight or bishop.

Fianchetto: the development of a bishop to b2, g2, b7 or g7.

Flight Square: an escape square to which an attacked piece, often a king, may run.

Initiative: a player has the initiative when he begins to play forcefully and restrict his opponent's choice of replies.

Kingside: the half of the board to White's right: the e-, f-, g- and h-files.

Loose: a piece that is undefended.

Major Pieces: the queens and rooks.

Material: a general term covering both pieces and pawns.

Minor Pieces: the bishops and knights.

Queenside: the half of the board to White's left: the a-, b-, c- and d-files.

Sacrifice: voluntarily giving up material in the hope of gaining some other kind of advantage.

1 The Basic Mates

Checkmate is the aim of the game. If you are starting out in chess, you will need to know the simple methods of mating your opponent when he has only his king left on the board. As you get stronger, you will find that your opponents will usually resign and not put you to the test. Even so, there will be times, particularly in quickplay events, where you are short of time and your opponent plays on. Then you will have to have a sound and reliable method that you can follow at speed before your flag falls.

The basic mates with queen or rook are easy. Those with the minor pieces are much more difficult, but don't worry too much about them. In fifty years of playing chess, I have never been asked to checkmate with bishop and knight or with two bishops. Nor have I ever seen a player having to do so.

1 Mate with King and Queen

Trap the king in his coffin and nail the lid shut! Here's how:

a) Use your queen to make the coffin smaller and smaller.

b) Use your king to give support.

c) Trap the enemy against the side of the board.

d) *But beware stalemate!*

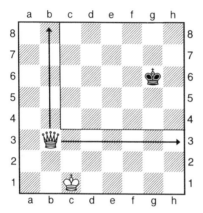

In this diagram the black king is trapped by the queen inside the rectangle of thirty squares shown. This is his coffin. You must make the rectangle smaller:

1 ♕d5 *(D)*

Look at the next diagram and see how this queen move has cut the black king's rectangle down to just twelve squares.

From now on you follow the simple method:

a) If you can make the rectangle smaller without it being stalemate, then do so.

b) If you can't make the rectangle smaller, bring up your king in support. By using your king and queen in combination, you will easily be able to make the rectangle smaller.

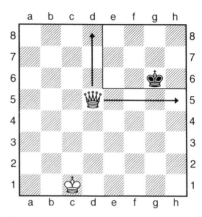

There are several moves the black king can make. It doesn't matter which; our method is just the same. Let's suppose:

1 ...   ♚f6 *(D)*

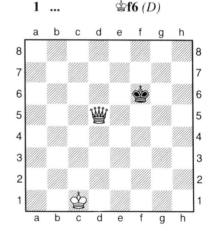

What now?

Can you make the rectangle smaller?

No.

Should you give check, by 2 ♕d6+ for instance?

No. Check is usually a bad idea because it lets the black king out of his coffin.

So, bring up your king!

2 ♔d2

The king has a long and slow journey to make. But there is no hurry. You have fifty moves in which to deliver checkmate, so the king will get there in plenty of time.

2 ... **♚g6**

3 ♕e5

Of course! White must make the rectangle smaller.

3 ... **♚f7**

4 ♔e3 **♚g6**

5 ♔f4 **♚f7**

6 ♔g5 *(D)*

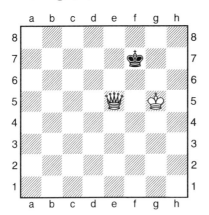

The black king has only two squares, f8 and g8, and he's going to be trapped on the edge of the board whichever he uses.

But as the king gets squashed into a smaller and smaller space, remember *stalemate*!

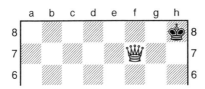

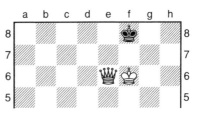

Beware of these two positions. Black has no legal move in either, so if it is his turn to move it is stalemate and the game is drawn. A silly way to lose half a point!

Now back to the play...

6 ... **♚g8**

Or 6...♚f8 7 ♔g6 ♚g8 and either 8 ♕g7# or 8 ♕e8#.

7 ♕e7

Now the black king is shut inside a rectangle of just two squares and nailing the lid on the coffin is easy.

7 ... **♚h8**

8 ♔g6 **♚g8**

9 ♕g7# *(D)*

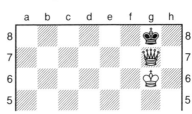

Or

9 ♕e8# *(D)*

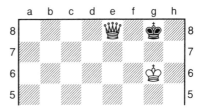

2 Mate with King and Rook

The method here is just the same as mating with king and queen.

a) Use your rook to make a rectangle.

b) Use your king to give support to the rook.

With a rook, the process is slower but the good news is that you don't have to worry quite so much about stalemate.

If it is Black's turn to move in the two positions below then he is stalemated.

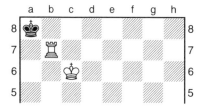

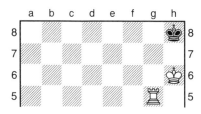

If you follow the mating method you are unlikely to reach either of these positions. *But remember:*

It is very easy when playing chess to get excited and carried away with your own plans, especially when you are winning. You must always remember your opponent is still there and every time you are about to move you must ask yourself the question 'What will he do next?'

We will start from the position in the following diagram:

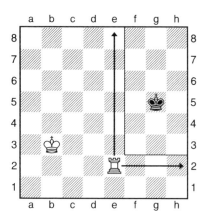

At first sight following our method it looks as if you should play 1 ♖e4 *(D)* and make the rectangle smaller.

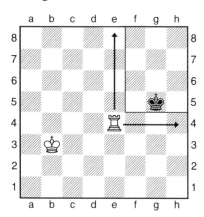

However, this does not bring you closer to your goal. Black will simply play 1...♔f5 and your rook will have to run away. The rook is not as powerful as the queen, and it is going to need more support from your king.

Remember that if we can't make the rectangle smaller then we bring the king up in support:

1   ♔c3   ♔f4

2 ♔d3   ♚f3
3 ♖e4 *(D)*

And now the black king is trapped inside a rectangle at White's end of the board.

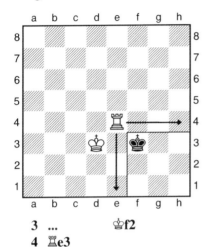

3 ...   ♚f2
4 ♖e3

You make the rectangle smaller.

4 ...   ♚g2
5 ♔e2 *(D)*

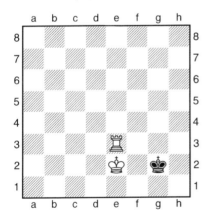

Your king and rook work together to squash the king into his coffin.

5 ...   ♚g1

6 ♖g3+   ♚h1
7 ♔f2   ♚h2 *(D)*

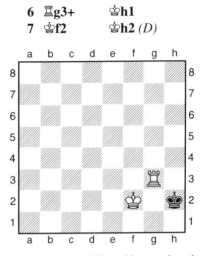

What to do now? Your king and rook are in perfect position but before you can give checkmate you must waste a move:

8 ♖e3

Or 8 ♖f3 or 8 ♖a3 – or any other rook move that doesn't let the black king escape from his corner.

8 ...   ♚h1

Black had only one possible move.

9 ♖h3# *(D)*

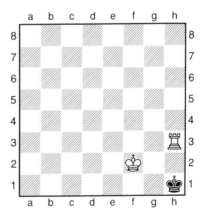

3 Mate with Two Rooks

This is the easiest of the basic mates.

a) Choose on which edge of the board you will mate the enemy king. (It won't matter which.)

b) First use one rook to prevent the king from escaping in the opposite direction.

c) Then use the rooks alternately to drive the king to its death on the edge.

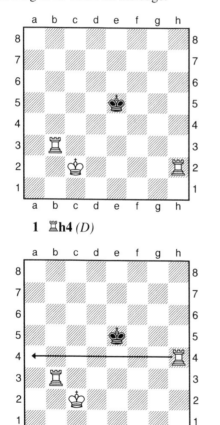

1 ℤh4 *(D)*

We have decided to mate the king on his own back line and your rook has moved to h4 to stop him escaping down the board.

1 ...   ♚d5
2 ℤb5+ *(D)*

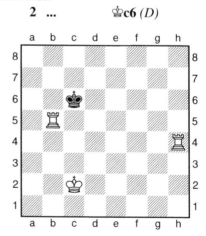

Your h4-rook prevents the king's escape and your b5-rook checks him and forces him backwards.

2 ...   ♚c6 *(D)*

The next logical step in our method would be to play 3 ℤh6+ but this allows 3...♚xb5. Not a good idea! Before you can play ℤh6+ you must first solve the problem of your b5-rook.

Move it!

Yes, but where to?

The rook must remain on the fifth rank, where he is stopping the king from coming back down the board. So, move him sideways as far away from the black king as you can without getting in the way of your other rook.

3 ♖g5 (D)

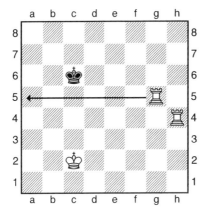

Problem solved! The rook is safe on g5 and the other rook is ready to move forward.

(Notice that if you had moved the rook further away from the king, to h5, your rooks would be on the same file getting in each other's way and you would not be able to play the rook from h4 to h6.)

3 ...   ♚d6

4 ♖h6+

Your rooks work as a team, one blocking the king's escape, the other checking and driving him back.

4 ...   ♚e7

5 ♖g7+   ♚f8 (D)

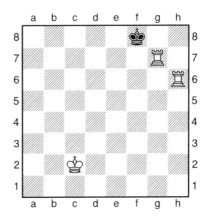

Now unfortunately 6 ♖h8+ allows Black to play 6...♚xg7 so again your rooks need repositioning.

6 ♖a7   ♚g8

7 ♖b6 (D)

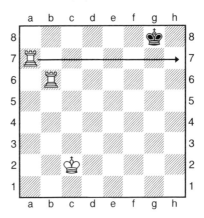

Your a7-rook is stopping the black king escaping from his back line so he is powerless against your next move:

8 ♖b8#

4 Mate with Two Bishops

This is a lot easier than it looks!

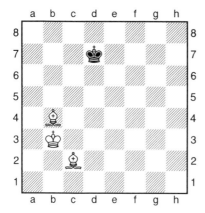

Your first step is to place your two bishops side by side.

  1 ♗e4   ♚e6
  2 ♗c3   ♚d6
  3 ♗d4 *(D)*

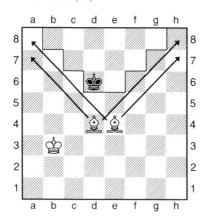

Step one accomplished! The two bishops stand proudly together side by side.

The black king cannot cross the arrowed diagonals, nor can he advance and attack the bishops. He is trapped in a box consisting of 12 squares.

Your second step is to push the black king backwards.

  3 **...**   ♚e6
  4 ♔c4

The white king lends a helping hand in forcing the black king towards the edge of the board.

  4 **...**   ♚d6
  5 ♗d5   ♚d7
  6 ♗e5   ♚e7
  7 ♔c5   ♚d7
  8 ♗d6   ♚d8
  9 ♗e6 *(D)*

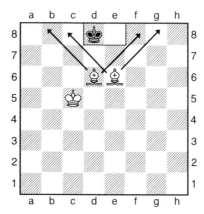

Step two accomplished. The two bishops still stand proudly side by side and your king has arrived to support them. The black king is still unable to cross the arrowed diagonals and now he is pinned to the edge of the board.

Your third step is to drive the king into the corner and checkmate him.

  9 **...**   ♚e8
  10 ♔c6   ♚d8
  11 ♗f7 *(D)*

You drive the king into the corner by preventing him from going the other way.

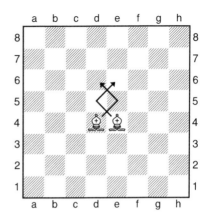

11	...	♚c8
12	♗e7	♚b8
13	♔b6	

Not 13 ♗e6 ♚a7. You must keep the king trapped on his back rank.

13	...	♚c8
14	♗e6+	♚b8
15	♗d6+	♚a8
16	♗d5# *(D)*	

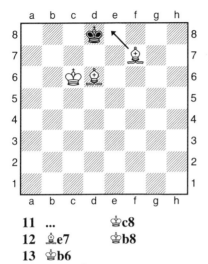

Notice the movement of the bishops from move five to move nine. They made a zigzag pattern:

This is the key to the second step. The bishops zigzag one square at a time up the board whilst their king gives support. Each time the bishops move up, the enemy king is confined in a smaller and smaller space. Finally the king is driven to a corner and mated.

Try for Yourself 1

Set up this position and see if you can checkmate the black king:

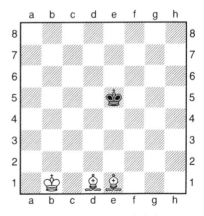

(You'll find one way of doing it on page 18.)

5 Mate with Bishop and Knight

It is very unlikely you will ever have to mate with bishop and knight in a real game, but if you do, these are the points to remember:

a) You will checkmate the king in a corner. If you have a light-squared bishop you will need to drive the king to h1 or a8. If your bishop is dark-squared then you will need to drive the king to a1 or h8.

b) All three of your pieces will need to work together, building a box to trap the king, stopping him from escaping and driving him into the corner.

c) In order to make things as awkward as possible, the enemy king will attempt to run away into the opposite colour corner to your bishop. This doesn't matter. Let him run! You will trap him in this corner and then drive him across the board into the same colour corner as your bishop.

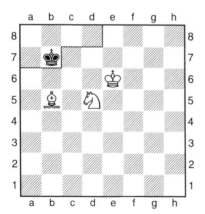

In this position we are well on the way to checkmate as the king is trapped in a box in the light-coloured corner. Now as usual you make the box smaller.

    1   ♞d7   ♚b8

    2   ♗a6 *(D)*

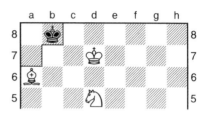

The black king is trapped in a triangle of squares.

    2   ...   ♚a7

    3   ♗c8

You save your bishop and keep the king trapped.

    3   ...   ♚b8

    4   ♞e7   ♚a7

    5   ♚c7

Now the black king's prison has been reduced to only two squares...

    5   ...   ♚a8

    6   ♗b7+   ♚a7

    7   ♞c6# *(D)*

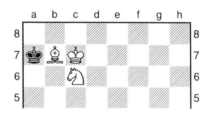

...and now he has none at all!

Try for Yourself 2

Suppose instead of 1...♚b8 Black had played 1...♚a7. How do you force mate? (One answer is on page 18.)

Now you have seen the finishing stages we must go back to the beginning! Take a look at the position at the top of the next page.

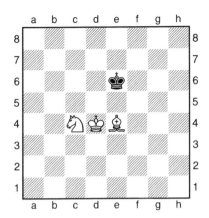

The white pieces are grouped together as a barrier in the centre of the board. Now you must try to drive the king to a corner.

    1 ♔c5   **♚f6**
    2 ♔d5   **♚f7**

The black king heads for h8. If 2...♚g5, then 3 ♔e5 ♚g4 4 ♔f6 and you drive him where he doesn't want to go, h1.

    3 ♔e5   **♚g7**
    4 ♔e6   **♚f8**
    5 ♔f6   **♚g8**

If 5...♚e8 you play 6 ♔g7 ♚e7 7 ♗d5 and the black king is already on his journey to a8.

    6 ♘e5   **♚h8** *(D)*

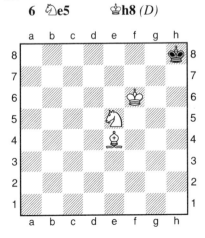

The black king has escaped to the wrong corner. No problem! You simply drive him across to a8.

    7 ♘f7+   **♚g8**
    8 ♗f5!

Often you will have to make little moves that don't actually threaten anything! This bishop leaves the black king with no choice other than to go in the direction he does not want to go.

    8 ...   **♚f8**
    9 ♗h7!   **♚e8**
    10 ♘e5 *(D)*

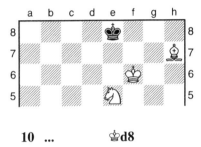

    10 ...   **♚d8**

Try for Yourself 3

Suppose Black had played 10...♚f8 instead. Can you force checkmate from this position? (You will find the quickest solution on page 18.)

Now back to the play:

    11 ♔e6   **♚c7**
    12 ♘d7   **♚c6**
    13 ♗d3!

Your bishop and knight keep the black king trapped in the corner.

    13 ...   **♚c7**
    14 ♗b5   **♚d8**
    15 ♘b6   **♚c7**
    16 ♘d5+   **♚b7**

And you have reached the position we started with on the previous page!

6 Mate with Two Knights

You needn't worry at all about how to force mate with two knights. Because you can't!

Here's why.

Knights control squares, not lines. Unlike the queen, the rook and the bishop, whenever knights move, they lose control over all the squares they were previously guarding. While king and two knights can drive the lone king near a corner, they cannot trap him in the corner itself without giving stalemate or allowing him to escape.

There are possible checkmate positions when the king is at the edge of the board, but your opponent has to make a really silly mistake to allow you to mate him. In fact, he can only lose if he overlooks a mate in one!

Look at this position:

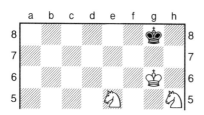

White can play **1 ♘f6+** and if the black king goes to h8 then **2 ♘f7# (D)** is mate.

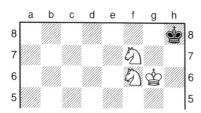

But why should the black king go to h8 when he can happily go to f8 and escape out into the middle of the board?

Try for Yourself Solutions

1) Here is one way the game might end. Notice the zigzag route of the bishops:

1 ♗d2 ♔d4 2 ♗e2 ♔e4 3 ♔c2 ♔d4 4 ♗d3 ♔d5 5 ♗e3 ♔e5 6 ♔c3 ♔d5 7 ♗d4 ♔c6 8 ♗c4 ♔d6 9 ♔b4 ♔c6 10 ♗c5 ♔c7 11 ♗d5 ♔d7 12 ♔b5 ♔c7 13 ♗c6 ♔d8 14 ♗d6 ♔c8 15 ♔b6 ♔d8

We have completed step two of the method and now we have to drive the king into the corner. We want to be able to play ♗e7 when the black king is on c8. This means 'wasting' a move somewhere with the bishop.

16 ♗b4 ♔c8 17 ♗e7 ♔b8 18 ♗d7 ♔a8

Now because 19 ♗d6 is stalemate we must 'waste' another move.

19 ♗g5 ♔b8 20 ♗f4+ ♔a8 21 ♗c6#

2) It's mate in five: **1...♔a7 2 ♔c7 ♔a8 3 ♘e7 ♔a7 4 ♘c8+ ♔a8 5 ♗c6#.**

3) **10...♔f8 11 ♘d7+ ♔e8 12 ♔e6 ♔d8 13 ♔d6 ♔e8 14 ♗g6+ ♔d8 15 ♘c5 ♔c8 16 ♗f7!**

White 'wastes' a move! If he plays 16 ♔c6 straightaway, then 16...♔d8 17 ♘b7+ ♔e7 and the king escapes.

16...♔d8 17 ♘b7+ ♔c8 18 ♔c6

Now there is no escape.

18...♔b8 19 ♔b6 ♔c8 20 ♗e6+ ♔b8

White need only deliver the final blow.

21 ♘a5

Or 21 ♘d8.

21...♔a8 22 ♗c8 ♔b8 23 ♗a6

Another 'wasted' move since 23 ♗b7?? would be stalemate!

23...♔a8 24 ♗b7+ ♔b8 25 ♘c6#

2 Tactical Themes

Tactics are fun! They are little tricks or traps – weapons which you can use to catch out your opponent and win his pieces or even checkmate him. A string of moves that involve a tactical theme is called a *combination*.

Tactics are fun because there is a great sense of pleasure when you catch out an opponent with something he hasn't seen.

You will find tactical themes in the problems or puzzles published in books, newspapers and magazines. It is a good idea to try to solve them. You will get a sense of pleasure when you do so and the practice will give you great ideas that you can use in your own games.

7 Decoy and Deflection

Mikhail Botvinnik's game against Jose Raul Capablanca at the AVRO tournament of 1938 is one of the most famous games in chess history – and mostly because of one move.

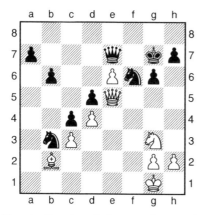

Botvinnik played the startling **1 ♗a3!!** and the game continued **1...♕xa3 2 ♘h5+!** (a second surprising sacrifice to expose the black king) **2...gxh5 3 ♕g5+ ♔f8 4 ♕xf6+ ♔g8 5 e7** *(D)*, reaching this position:

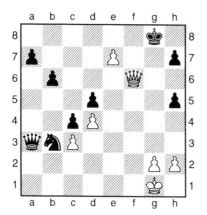

Botvinnik's bishop has lured the black queen away from her king. It *deflected* her

from where she needed to be. Capablanca's king was left alone and defenceless. He had a few checks with his own queen but when these ran out he had to resign as he had no pieces with which to defend his king:

5...♕c1+ 6 ♔f2 ♕c2+ 7 ♔g3 ♕d3+ 8 ♔h4 ♕e4+ 9 ♔xh5 ♕e2+ 10 ♔h4 ♕e4+ 11 g4 ♕e1+ 12 ♔h5

and Capablanca resigned.

You must always be on the lookout for ways of luring pieces away from good defensive squares.

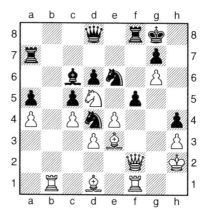

In this position Botvinnik, playing White against Paul Keres at the Soviet team championship in Moscow in 1966, realized if he could play ♕xh4 he would force mate on the h-file.

The problem is that Black's queen on d8 is defending h4.

Question: How to get rid of the black queen?

Answer: *Deflect* her, force her away from the defence of the h4-pawn!

1 ♖b8!! *(D)*

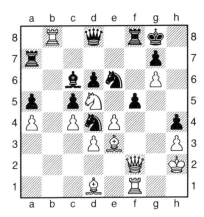

The black queen is attacked so she can't stay where she is and she will be gobbled up by a white minor piece if she goes to e7, f6 or g5. 1...♕xb8 allows 2 ♕xh4 so Keres resigned.

In the position below Lustrov, playing Black against Ivanovsky in Moscow in 1972, realized the white king is not as safe as he seems.

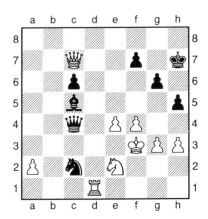

Indeed if he could get rid of the rook on d1, ...♘e1 would be mate.

A sacrifice is needed to *deflect* the white rook:

1...♕d3+!! 2 ♖xd3 ♘e1# (D)

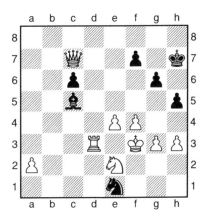

Try for Yourself 4

When you see that a powerful move is prevented by a defender, find a way of dealing with that defender. Ludolf did just that as White in his game with Kots in Leningrad 1962.

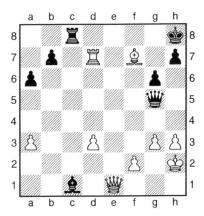

The first step is to work out where you would like White's queen to be. Then you should look for the move that will help you get her there.

(The solution is on page 38.)

8 Double Attacks and Forks

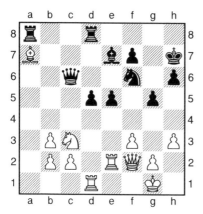

This is a position from a game between Engels and Stantić at Nova Gorica 2000.

Black surprised his opponent by playing **1...♖xa7!**.

Why? A rook is worth more than a bishop, and surely White can capture the rook with **2 ♕xa7**?

Yes, but then he is hit by Black's reply **2...♗c5+!** *(D)*.

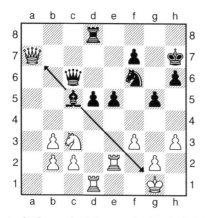

A *fork* or *double attack*! Both White's king and his queen are under attack. Whatever White plays, he will lose his queen.

You should always be on the lookout for loose pieces in the enemy camp. Paul Morphy, the great American champion of the 19th century, was quick to spot his chance against Mongredien in Paris in 1859:

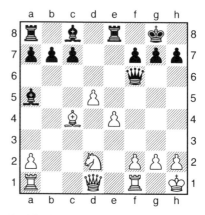

The black rook on e8 and the bishop on a5 are both loose so Morphy *forked* them very simply with **1 ♕a4!** *(D)*.

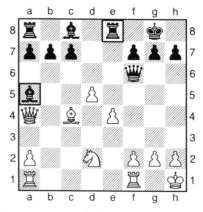

Queens are useful pieces for making double attacks as they hit in several directions at long range.

Knights are also good forking pieces. They can hit in all directions at seemingly unconnected squares. Their awkward crab-like move means that a knight fork often comes as a surprise – often as the sting in the tail of a combination.

The next position, from a game played by correspondence between Karafaieth and Kliesch in 1973, is a good example of the knight appearing from nowhere to hit two apparently unconnected squares:

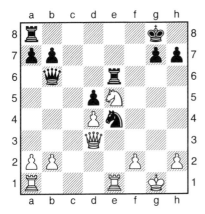

Black played **1...♖xe5!**. Why? After **2 dxe5 ♕xf2+ 3 ♔h1** *(D)* the king has run away into the corner and White seems to have survived...

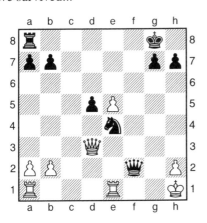

...but now comes the sting: **3...♕xe1+! 4 ♖xe1 ♘f2+** *(D)* and Black regains the queen and remains a piece ahead.

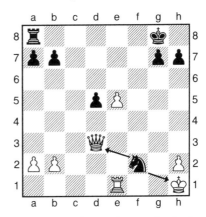

You should always be on the lookout for target or *forking* squares, especially when your knight is aggressively placed.

Try for Yourself 5

In the game Nemet vs Giertz at Basle 2000 White spotted a target square for a knight *fork*:

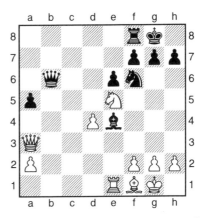

Can you spot the target square and work out the sequence of moves which won material for Nemet?

(The answer is on page 38.)

9 Discovered Attacks

What do you notice about the position of the two queens in the game Timman vs Andersson at Tilburg 1984?

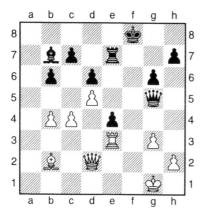

Both queens are on the same diagonal.

Both queens are undefended.

Only the white rook stands between them. When White moves his rook, the diagonal will be open, so:

1 ♖f3+!! *(D)*

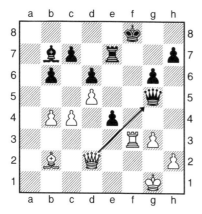

Yes, the rook is *en prise* ... but so is the black queen! The rook move has *discovered* an attack by White's queen on Black's queen.

Andersson resigned because he will lose queen for rook.

Discovering an attack and particularly *discovering check* allows a piece to venture where it would not normally dare to go. The well-known Petroff Defence opening trap is a good example:

1 e4 e5 2 ♘f3 ♘f6 3 ♘xe5 ♘xe4?! 4 ♕e2 ♘f6??

Now any move by the white knight will open the line from the white queen on e2 to the black king on e8 – it will *discover check*.

Question: where should the white knight go?

Answer: where it can do most damage!

5 ♘c6+! *(D)*

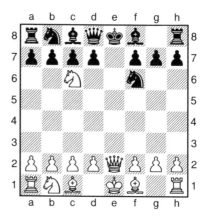

Yes, the knight is *en prise* but Black has to get out of check. He doesn't have time to take the knight and he will lose his queen next move.

You must always be on the lookout for the chance of opening the line of attack for a queen, a rook or a bishop.

The next position could have arisen in a game Lein vs Polugaevsky at the Soviet

Championship in Tbilisi in 1966/7, if Polugaevsky had not resigned first:

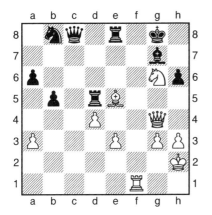

White has sacrificed a rook. Why?

Because he realized that if his knight disappeared from g6 he could deliver mate by ♕xg7#.

Lein's idea was based on two tactical themes:

1 ♘e7+!! *(D)*

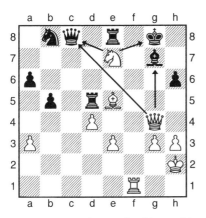

There's a lot going on in this position!

The knight move has discovered the threat of 2 ♕xg7#.

The knight move is also check and a double attack – it is forking Black's king and queen.

If Black plays 1...♖xe7 he seems to solve both problems. He's captured the knight and from e7 his rook is guarding g7 against the mate threat.

However, Black has a third problem! His rook is needed on e8 to defend his queen. The fact that it must take the white knight deflects it from this vital function: 1...♖xe7 allows 2 ♕xc8+ ♔h7 3 ♕xb8.

Try for Yourself 6

This position is from the game Bonch-Osmolovsky vs Ragozin at Lvov 1951.

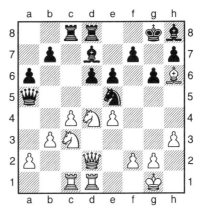

Which of Black's pieces could be in danger on the same line as a white piece? Which piece does White need to move to *discover* an attack? Where should the piece go to cause most damage?

(Answer on page 38.)

10 The Pin

In this position the black rook on e5 stands proudly in the middle of the board. Can you see why it might be in trouble?

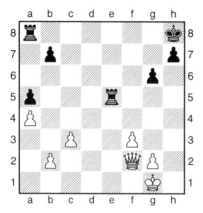

The rook stands on the same diagonal as its king. After **1 ♕d4** it is *pinned* to the spot. It is unable to move because the king would be in check if it did. Black can defend with **1...♖ae8** but then White will simply hit the rook with his pawn and there is no escape: **2 f4** *(D)*.

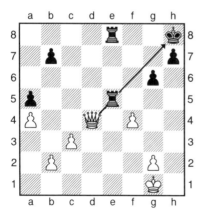

As well as looking for ways to attack and to win *pinned* pieces, you should remember that when a piece is *pinned* it loses its power to defend. In the game Cherniaev vs Beshukov at Hastings 1999/00. White's castled position looks sound...

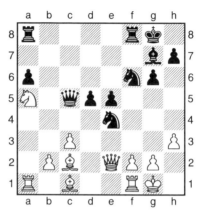

...but when we look closer we see that the pawn on f2 is *pinned* to its king by the black queen. The pawn *should* be defending g3. But it isn't! Black can play **1...♘g3!** *(D)* forking queen and rook.

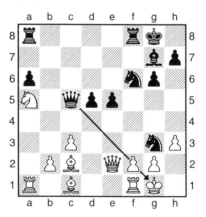

In both of the positions we have just seen, the *pinned* piece simply was not able to move.

In the next example the *pinned* piece *can* move – and this makes a big difference!

No doubt Ivashin, playing Black against Shamkovich at Gorky in 1946, thought that White could not move his f3-knight.

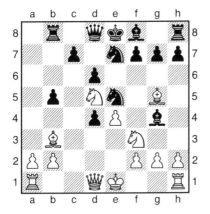

He was wrong! The knight *can* move and **1 ♘xe5** wins a piece since 1...♗xd1 2 ♘f6+ gxf6 3 ♗xf7# *(D)* is mate.

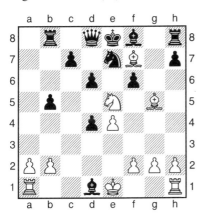

Ivashin tried **1...♘xd5 2 ♕xg4 f6 3 ♗xf6** before resigning.

This idea for breaking the *pin* came from a game by the French master Sire de Legall played in 1787: **1 e4 e5 2 ♘f3 d6 3 ♗c4 ♗g4 4 ♘c3 g6?** and Black was mated by **5 ♘xe5! ♗xd1 6 ♗xf7+ ♔e7 7 ♘d5#.**

You must remember that a *pin* is only a *total pin* when a piece is *pinned* against its king. Then it *cannot* move. If a piece is *pinned* against another piece then it *can* move even if it is usually not safe to do so.

Try for Yourself 7

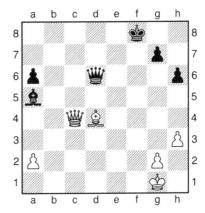

Finding the *pin* for White in this position from Brundtrup vs Budrich in Berlin 1954 is not too difficult, but winning is not quite as easy as that! You are going to have to look a bit further to find out how White wins.

(The solution is on page 38.)

11 The Skewer

Tan, playing Black against Mecking in the 1973 Petropolis Interzonal, was possibly quite happy with this position.

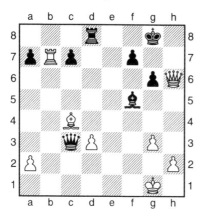

But then **1 ♗xf7+!** put an end to any state of happiness! Tan had no choice: he had to recapture with **1...♔xf7**, whereupon he was saddened further by the second sacrifice **2 ♖xc7+!** *(D)*.

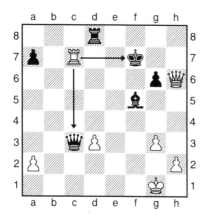

Tan's king and queen are forked so again he has no choice: **2...♕xc7**.

Now Mecking produced the killer move of his combination, **3 ♕h7+** *(D)*.

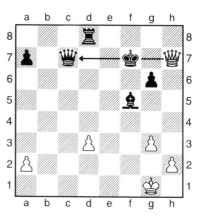

Tan's king and queen have been caught on the same line. They have been *skewered*. The king is in check. He must move. The queen will then be captured.

Mecking was very imaginative to realize that Black's king and queen would end up on the same rank.

You must be imaginative and visualize enemy pieces coming together on the same line!

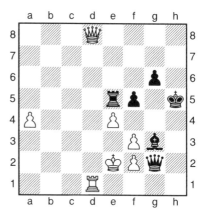

Think! Where would White like Black's queen to be in this position?

In the game Bena vs Ksarko in Romania in 1971 White lured Black's queen onto the h-file with **1 ♖h1+!!** (a *decoy* – the queen is lured to a fatal square) where she was promptly *skewered*: **1...♕xh1 2 ♕h8+** *(D)*.

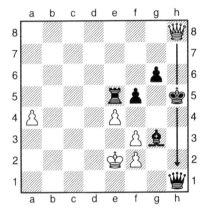

In the next example, Nigel Short spotted Rafael Vaganian's king and queen on the same diagonal in Barcelona in 1989.

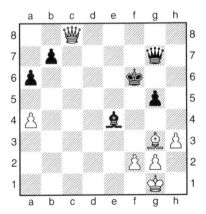

He realized that the immediate *skewer* 1 ♕c3+ would get nowhere as the king would side-step to g6 and defend the queen. So he lured the king forward with another *skewer*.

1 ♗e5+!! forces **1...♔xe5** and now **2 ♕c3+** *(D)* is a winning *skewer*.

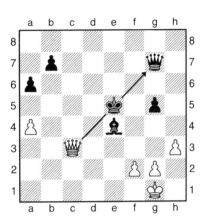

When the king moves, the black queen is lost.

Try for Yourself 8
Whenever you see two pieces on the same line you should always be thinking of pin and *skewer*.

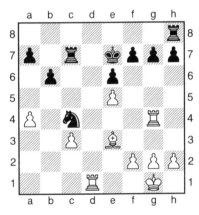

In this position which black pieces are loose? Is one of them on the same line as another piece? Can you see a possible *skewer* and what White must do to set it up?

The game is Espig vs Brüggemann from the 1973 East German Championship, played at Erfurt.

(The answer is on page 38.)

12 Interference or Line-Blocking

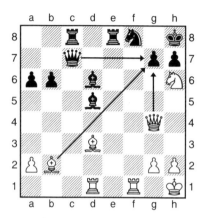

Najdorf, playing White against Matanović at Mar del Plata in 1961, has his eye on g7. Only the black queen on c7 is preventing the immediate 1 ♕xg7#.

Can the black queen be deflected away? No!

Question: How do you deal with her?

Answer: *Block her line* of defence!

1 ♘f7+ *(D)*

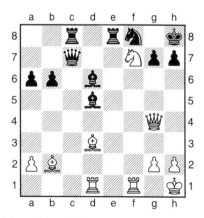

The white knight is *blocking the line* of the black queen from c7 to g7 so 1...♔g8 is answered by 2 ♕xg7#. Taking the knight

is no better: **1...♗xf7 2 ♕xg7#** *(D)* is still mate.

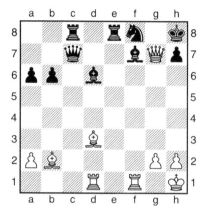

The f7-bishop *interferes* with the movement of the black queen. Her *line* to g7 is *blocked* and Black is mated.

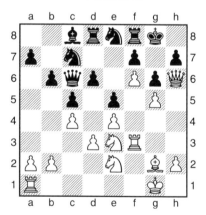

In this position Reshevsky, playing White against Persitz at Haifa in 1958, wants to play 1 ♖h3 and 2 ♕xh7#. He can't. There's a black bishop on c8 attacking h3.

Reshevsky cannot deflect the bishop away so he *blocked* its *line* with **1 ♘f5** and Persitz resigned, because after **1...♗xf5** (1...gxf5 is answered immediately with 2 ♖h3) **2 exf5** *(D)* Black will have to give up his queen to prevent 3 ♖h3 followed by mate with the queen on h7.

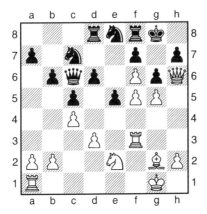

You should always be on the lookout for ways of dealing with enemy defensive pieces.

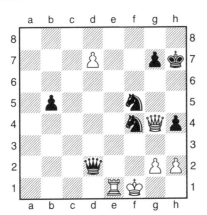

Burlage forgot this when here he played 1...♕xd7 and went on to lose to Happel at Wijk aan Zee in 2000.

Burlage must have seen that 1...♕xg2+ would be mate if it were not for White's

defending queen on g4, but he missed the chance to *interfere* with the defender.

1...♘g3+ would have *blocked the line* and after **2 hxg3** (or 2 ♔g1), **2...♕xg2#** *(D)* is mate.

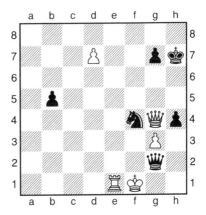

The white queen's line to g2 is blocked.

Try for Yourself 9

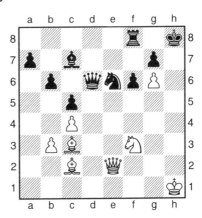

Can you see which black piece is the annoying defender in this position and how White deals with it?

(The answer is on page 38.)

13 The Intermezzo

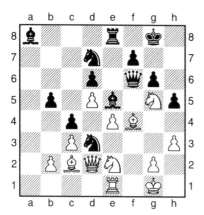

This position comes from a game between John Emms and Peter Wells at the 1989 British Championship in Plymouth.

Emms played **1 ♗xe5** *(D)*, capturing the bishop and attacking Black's queen.

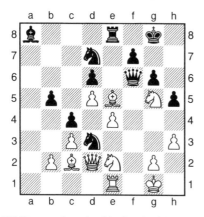

Wells was faced with the decision of how to recapture. Both of his knights, his queen, his rook and his d-pawn can take the bishop. What move do you think Black should play?

Wells considered his options, decided on 1...♖xe5 ... and immediately realized that he had made a mistake!

He didn't have to capture on e5 at all. He had a far better move! He could have played **1...♕f2+** *(D)*.

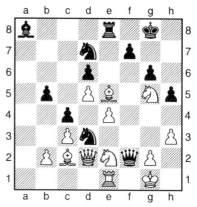

After **2 ♔h1** (or 2 ♔h2) **2...♘xe1** *(D)* White has to give up his queen to avoid mate on g2.

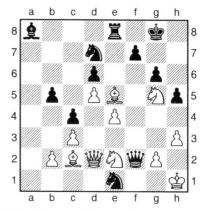

Why did two of England's brightest young players, both to become grandmasters, miss something so obvious?

The move **1...♕f2+** is an *intermezzo*, an in-between move. Both players were concentrating on the point of action, the square e5, and this concentration took their minds off other things.

If you walk into any clubroom or tournament hall you will see players instinctively making recaptures or *obvious* moves without any thought at all. Usually their decisions will be correct but sometimes the position will contain an *in-between move* that they haven't even looked for!

When you have found a good move, have a quick look for a better one! Don't waste clock time, but do avoid responding automatically.

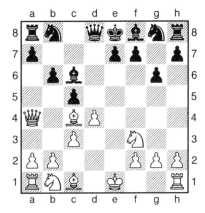

In this position Kantorovich has just played 1...♗c6, attacking Aronin's queen in their game at the Soviet team championship in Moscow in 1960.

Kantorovich naturally assumed that since the queen was attacked she would have to move. He didn't look for anything else and was stunned by **2 ♘e5!** *(D)* forking the c6-bishop and mate on f7. Black has to deal with the threat of mate, but however he does this he will lose some material because of White's other threats.

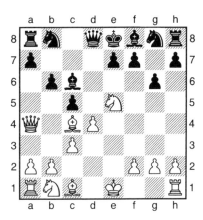

Kantorovich soon had to resign. He paid the price for not looking any further than the obvious. The thought of an *intermezzo* had not entered his head.

Try for Yourself 10

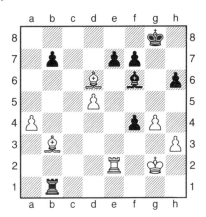

Sherwin, playing Black here against Rossetto at the Portorož Interzonal in 1958, seems to have a choice. He can regain his piece by 1...exd6 or 1...♖xb3. Which is better?

Which bishop should Black take?

(Answer on page 38.)

14 Perpetual Check

Sutovsky, playing Black, had sacrificed a piece to open up Rowson's king's position in their game at the Isle of Man tournament in 1999 but his attack had apparently ground to a halt.

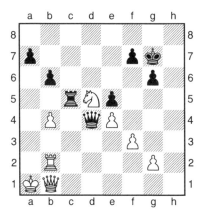

White's king seems safe and Sutovsky has no obvious compensation for the piece he has sacrificed. Sutovsky played **1...♖a5+! 2 bxa5 ♕a4+** *(D)*.

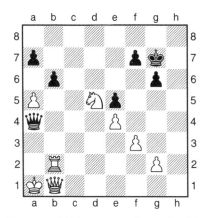

How can White escape from check?

Rowson tried **3 ♕a2** and was promptly checked again by **3...♕d1+**. He put his rook

in the way with **4 ♖b1** but the queen found another check, **4...♕d4+** *(D)*.

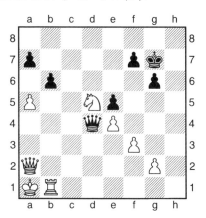

The game was agreed drawn. The black queen has a triangle of squares, a4, d4 and d1, and White cannot escape the checks. However White blocks one check, the black queen will always have another square from which to give check again. She can go on giving check for ever: *perpetual check*.

5 ♘c3 ♕xc3+ *(D)* doesn't help either.

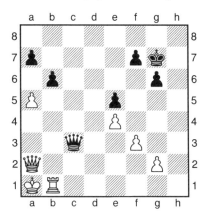

The black queen still has a *perpetual check*, this time using the squares a5, c3 and e1.

You should remember that half a point is better than nothing! If your attack has run out of steam, look for a way of cutting your losses.

Knowing that you have a *perpetual check* can also enable you to be brave. Imagine you are attacking. You see that you can sacrifice pieces to smash away the king's defences. But are you winning? There are a lot of variations. It's complicated. You are not sure. If you can see that you have *at least a draw* by *perpetual check* it may be worth going ahead with the attack. You can look for ways of winning as you go along knowing that you won't lose!

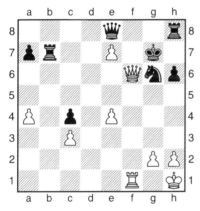

Here, P. Ornstein had done just that. He had invested a rook and knight in his attack against T. Svensen at Gausdal 2000.

Ornstein had not been able to find a way to win but he was happy because he knew he could draw by perpetual check: 1...♔g8 2 ♕e6+ ♔g7 3 ♕f6+, etc.

Ornstein was happier still when Svensen cracked under the pressure of the attack and played **1...♔h7?**, allowing **2 ♕f7+ ♕xf7 3 ♖xf7+ ♔g8 4 e8♕+** *(D)*.

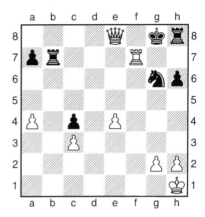

It is mate next move!

Try for Yourself 11

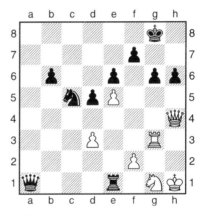

Vitoliņš was three pawns down with no obvious compensation in his game with Bukhman at Riga in 1976. How did he save himself from this desperate situation?

Perpetual check of course ... but how?

(The answer is on page 38.)

15 Stalemate

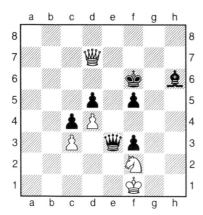

This position is from Kljako vs Vezzosi at Martigny in 1988.

Vezzosi would have calculated that he could avoid perpetual check. No doubt he was expecting to win the endgame with his two extra pawns. He was not expecting the continuation **1 ♘g4+!! fxg4 2 ♕f5+! ♚xf5** *(D)*.

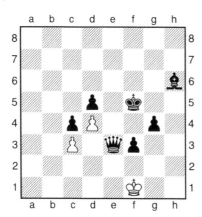

Stalemate! Vezzosi is a queen, bishop and two pawns ahead but White's king has no legal move and his pawns are all blocked. Draw!

Let's look again at what happened. Vezzosi had to play 1...fxg4 because his king and queen were forked. But he didn't have to continue 2...♚xf5. He could have played 2...♚g7 or 2...♚e7. In both cases White simply chases after the king with his queen until Black is forced to capture her with his king. For example, 2...♚e7 3 ♕f7+ ♚d6 4 ♕d7+ *(D)*.

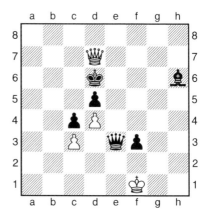

Now 4...♚xd7 is forced and we have another *stalemate* position. Draw!

As we said with perpetual check, half a point is better than nothing! Normally it seems that *stalemate* is only likely to arise when one player has just his king and perhaps a pawn or two left on the board. Yet the above example shows that you should be alert all the time. Often a *stalemating* move will come completely out of the blue.

In our next position Murey (playing Black) caught Titenko with just such a stunning move in Moscow 1963.

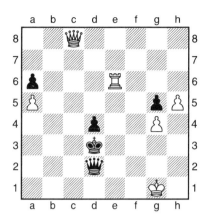

A rook down and with no hope of perpetual check after 1...♛d1+ 2 ♔h2 ♛d2+ 3 ♔h3, Murey discovered the way to draw: **1...♛c1+!**. Murey's queen is forking king and queen so **2 ♛xc1** *(D)* is forced.

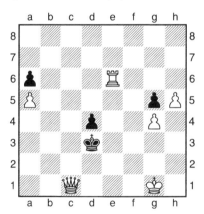

Stalemate. Black does not have a legal move. Draw! Murey has saved himself.

In every position when you are planning your move, you should be asking yourself the question 'What will he do next?' If you do this in simple endgame positions you will never blunder into a silly *stalemate*.

But as you have seen, *stalemate* can sometimes arise when there are still several pieces on the board ... you have to be alert to this possibility!

The clues to look out for are blocked pawns and a king without space. Then achieving stalemate is a matter of sacrificing the remaining pieces.

Try for Yourself 12

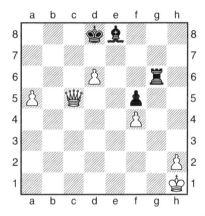

This position is from the game Fichtl vs F. Blatny at Bratislava 1956. Thinking that he was winning easily, White has just played 1 d6??. How does Black save himself?

(The answer is on page 38.)

Try for Yourself Solutions

4)

If White could put his queen somewhere on the long a1-h8 diagonal it would be mate. How to get her there? White cannot play 1 ♕c3+ ♖xc3 or 1 ♕e5+ ♕xe5 straight away so Ludolf played the deflecting move **1 ♖d8+!!** first. Now both 1...♖xd8 2 ♕c3+ and 1...♕xd8 2 ♕e5+ lead to mate, so Kots resigned.

5)

d7 is the target square so first Nemet deflected the f6-knight: **1 ♖xe4 ♘xe4**. Now the obvious 2 ♘d7 fork gets nowhere due to 2...♕b4 3 ♕xb4 axb4 4 ♘xf8 ♔xf8, so Nemet played **2 ♕xf8+! ♔xf8 3 ♘d7+** and came out a piece up.

6)

On a5 the black queen is loose and on the same line as White's queen. A move by the c3-knight will discover the attack. **1 ♘d5!** threatens 2 ♘e7#. If Black avoids the mate, he must leave his queen to be captured.

7)

White can pin the black queen to her king with **1 ♗c5** but Black has a pin of his own: **1...♗b6!**. It looks as though Black has escaped until we remember that Black's queen has lost her power of movement. White can now play **2 ♕f4+** forking king and queen. Black cannot play 2...♕xf4 so his queen is lost.

8)

If Black didn't have a pawn on f7 then 1 ♖xg7+ would be an immediate skewer and Black could resign. But Black does have a pawn on f7. So, get rid of it! After **1 ♗g5+**, **1...f6** is forced since 1...♔e8 2 ♖d8# is mate, but after **2 ♗xf6+!** Black resigned, since 2...gxf6 3 ♖g7+ costs him his c7-rook.

9)

White wants to play ♕h2+ and give mate on h7 so he has to deal with the problem of the black queen. He blocks her line spectacularly with **1 ♗e5!!**. Black cannot both save his queen and avoid mate. (Note that 1 ♘e5 allows the black king to escape by playing 1...♔g8.)

10)

Both of them! First Sherwin played the clever *intermezzo* **1...f3+!**. White's king and rook are forked and after **2 ♔xf3** the capture **2...♖xb3+** is *check*! After White moves out of check, Black has time to capture the second piece on d6.

11)

White needs to smash open the black king's position to get a perpetual check with his queen, but he has to be careful how he does it. The obvious 1 ♖xg6+ gets nowhere after 1...fxg6 2 ♕d8+ ♔f7 3 ♕c7+ ♔e8 4 ♕c8+ ♔e7 5 ♕c7+ ♘d7! 6 ♕d6+ ♔d8 because White has no more checks. To draw, White has to check first with the queen: **1 ♕d8+ ♔h7 2 ♖xg6**. Now 2...fxg6 3 ♕e7+ and 2...♔xg6 3 ♕f6+ ♔h5 4 ♕f3+ both leave Black unable to escape the checks.

12)

Firstly Black first gets rid of his bishop by **1...♗c6+ 2 ♕xc6** so that his king is tied up and he has only a rook which he can move. Secondly he gets rid of the rook: **2...♖g1+ 3 ♔xg1** stalemate!

3 Endgame Basics

Before you turn over the page, remember two things:

a) You can be winning a game in the opening. You can be winning in the middlegame. But no matter how well you have played, you can still mess everything up in the endgame.

b) There are only a few pieces on the board so at first glance endgame positions seem simple. They may be simple, but the problem is that you have to play with great accuracy. One small error can be fatal.

16 The Opposition

Set up this position on your board.

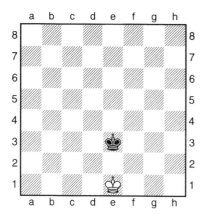

Let's suppose that White wants to get his king to the far end of the board, to any square on the eighth rank.

Can he get there?

Does it matter whose move it is?

Let's see. Suppose it is White's move.

The white king can't advance to f2, e2 or d2 because the black king is blocking or *opposing* him. The white king has to move sideways. Suppose **1 ♔d1**.

What does Black do?

1...♚d3! *(D)*

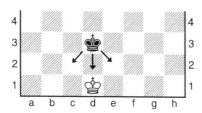

Of course! He continues to oppose the white king.

Every time the white king takes a step sideways the black king follows and opposes

him. The white king will never get off the first rank. We say that the black king has *the opposition*; he is stopping the white king from advancing.

Now let's suppose it is Black's turn to move in the original position.

The black king will either have to retreat or move sideways.

Suppose **1...♚d3** *(D)*.

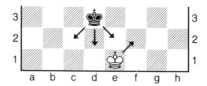

Black no longer has *the opposition*. He attacks e2, d2 and c2, but not f2. The white king can escape from the back rank and begin his charge up the board.

2 ♔f2 *(D)*

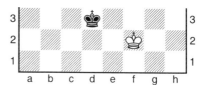

2...♚e4 3 ♔g3 ♚f5 4 ♔h4 ♚g6 *(D)*

The white king has hit the edge of the board. He seems to be blocked, but...

5 ♔g4 *(D)*

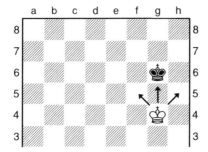

The white king has *the opposition*. He attacks h5, g5 and f5. The black king will have to give way again and White can continue his advance up the board. By repeating the same method again and again the white king will eventually reach the eighth rank.

Let's go back to the original position and suppose the black king retreats with **1...♚e4** *(D)*.

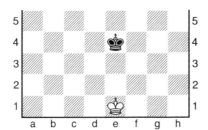

After this, which square should the white king go to?

Well, White does not want Black to gain *the opposition* and that is just what will happen after either 2 ♔f2 ♚f4 or 2 ♔d2 ♚d4.

White must keep the opposition for himself. He should play **2 ♔e2!** *(D)*.

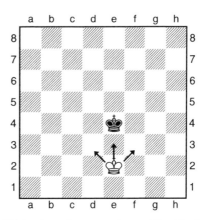

White has *the opposition*. The black king must give way and White can advance.

Having *the opposition* is often the difference between winning and drawing king and pawn endgames. Practise king vs king a few times yourself and make sure you understand the idea.

Try for Yourself 13

The white king is trying to get to the eighth rank.

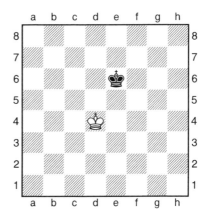

What will happen if Black plays:
a) 1...♚f6; b) 1...♚f7; c) 1...♚e7
d) 1...♚d7; e) 1...♚d6
(Answer on page 60.)

17 Promotion and the Opposition

Having *the opposition* is most important when trying to promote a pawn.

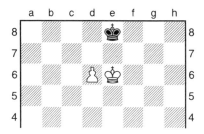

If it is Black's turn to move in this position then White has *the opposition* and White will win: **1...♔d8 2 d7 ♔c7 3 ♔e7** *(D)*.

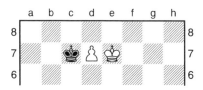

The white pawn will promote on the next move.

If it is White's turn to move in the original position then Black has *the opposition* and White will *not* win:

1 d7+ ♔d8 2 ♔d6 *(D)*

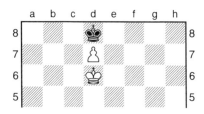

Stalemate! Black has no legal move, so the game is drawn.

Of course if it is White's move he does not have to play 1 d7+. He can try fiddling around with his king, hoping to lose a move. If he can return to the original position with *Black* to move, then White will win.

Black has to be careful!

He must not lose *the opposition*!

After **1 ♔e5 ♔d7 2 ♔d5** *(D)*, where should the black king go?

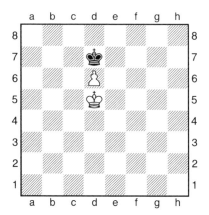

Black needs to keep *the opposition*. He will lose *the opposition* if he plays 2...♔e8 3 ♔e6 or if he plays 2...♔c8 3 ♔c6.

Black has to play **2...♔d8!** *(D)*.

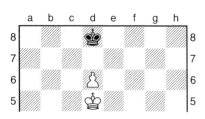

If White plays 3 ♔e6 Black keeps *the opposition* with 3...♔e8.

If White plays 3 ♔c6 Black keeps *the opposition* with 3...♔c8.

For Black, having *the opposition* is the difference between drawing and losing.

If the pawn has not already reached the sixth rank, the general rule is that to win you will need both:

a) to have *the opposition*.

b) to get your king in front of your pawn.

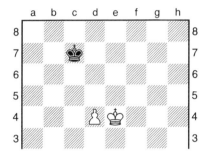

In this position if it is Black's turn to move he will draw: **1...♔d6 2 d5 ♔d7! 3 ♔e5 ♔e7 4 d6+ ♔d7 5 ♔d5 ♔d8** and we have the position in the last diagram on the previous page.

If it is White's turn to move he can win, but only if he plays **1 ♔e5 ♔d7** (if 1...♔c6, White wins with 2 ♔e6! and not with 2 d5+? ♔d7, which only draws) **2 ♔d5**, when he has gained the opposition and forces the black king to give way. **2...♔e7 3 ♔c6** *(D)*.

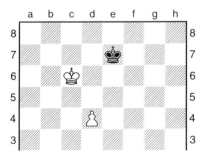

Black can only choose how to lose!

The variations **3...♔e6 4 d5+ ♔e7 5 ♔c7**, **3...♔e8 4 ♔c7 ♔e7 5 d5** and **3...♔d8 4 ♔d6 ♔e8 5 ♔c7 ♔e7 6 d5** all reach the following position:

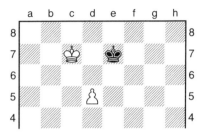

The white king shepherds the pawn to the queening square.

Try for Yourself 14

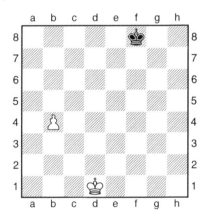

It is White's move in this study composed by Jan Drtina in 1908. Can White win?

Remember the rule: to promote the pawn, White must get his king in front of it and be able to gain the opposition.

(The solution is on page 60.)

18 The Rook's Pawn and Stalemate

In the diagram below White can get his king in front of his pawn. He may even gain the opposition. But he cannot win!

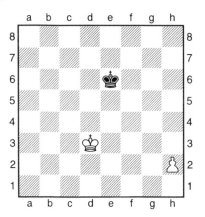

Let's play a few moves and see why Black can draw.

1 ♔e4 ♔f6 2 ♔f4 ♔g6 3 ♔g4 ♔h6 4 ♔h4 *(D)*

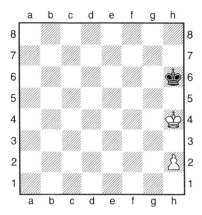

White has the opposition so the black king must give way:

4...♔g6 *(D)*

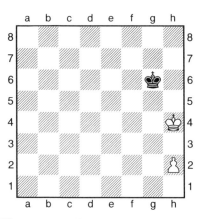

The move White wants to play now is 5 ♔i5, but sadly the square i5 does not exist!

White has hit the edge of the board and there's no way for his king to make progress.

Let's suppose White now continues trying to advance his king and pawn:

5 ♔g4 ♔h6 6 h4 ♔g6 7 h5+ ♔h6 8 ♔h4 ♔g7

Black has happily retreated with his king. He doesn't even have to worry about losing the opposition because **9 ♔g5 ♔h7 10 h6 ♔g8 11 ♔g6 ♔h8 12 h7** *(D)* is stalemate.

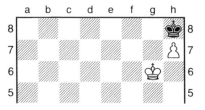

The square i7 does not exist either!

Once he is in the corner, the king is safe; the game will always end in stalemate.

19 The Wrong Bishop

In the diagram below White is not just a pawn ahead. He's got a bishop as well, but he still cannot win.

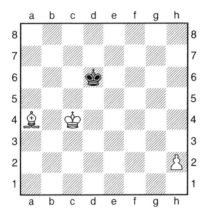

Let's play a few moves and see what happens: **1 ♔d4 ♚e6 2 ♔e4 ♚f6 3 ♔f4 ♚g6 4 ♔g4 ♚h6 5 h4 ♚g6 6 h5+ ♚h6 7 ♗c2 ♚g7 8 ♔g5 ♚g8 9 ♔g6 ♚h8 10 h6 ♚g8 11 ♗b3+ ♚h8** *(D)*.

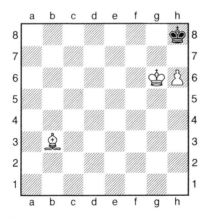

White cannot drive the king from his corner!

White's problem is that his bishop operates on *the wrong colour squares*.

To drive the king from the corner White needs a *dark-squared* bishop.

If his bishop stands on b4...

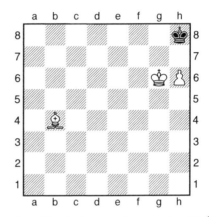

...he will win because he can play **12 ♗c3+ ♚g8 13 h7+** *(D)*.

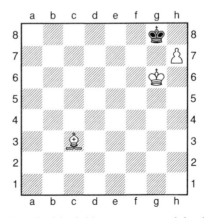

Now the black king cannot sneak back into his corner. The h8-square is under White's control and the pawn will promote.

20 The Rook's Pawn and the Trapped King

In the diagram below the black king cannot reach the blocking square h8.

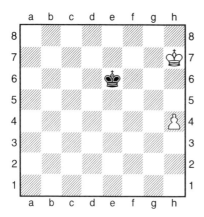

However, if it is Black's move, he can play **1...♔f7!** (D).

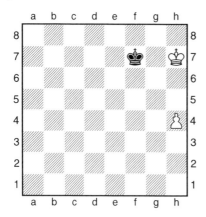

White now has a problem. Black has the *side opposition*! White's king cannot go to g6, g7 or g8 so he cannot get out of the way of his own pawn!

After **2 h5 ♔f8 3 h6 ♔f7 4 ♔h8 ♔f8** (D) White's king is trapped in the corner and he can only choose which way he wishes to draw:

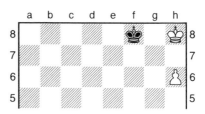

a) **5 ♔h7 ♔f7 6 ♔h8 ♔f8** and the kings can dance all night.

b) **5 h7 ♔f7** (D).

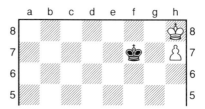

Now White has no legal move. Stalemate!

White's only way of getting his king out of the corner would have been on the third move. Instead of 3 h6 he could have played **3 ♔g6** (D).

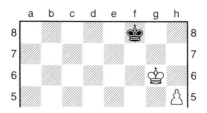

The white king has escaped but Black will grab the corner for his own king with **3...♔g8**, with a draw.

This all seems straightforward but as always in chess you have to be careful!

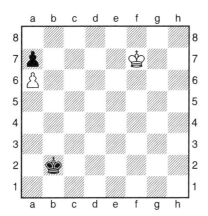

The plans for both sides are obvious. White's king will try to march across the board and snaffle the pawn on a7.

Black's king will try to march up the board and arrive on c7, where it will trap the white king in the corner.

Let's see what can happen:

1 ♔e7 ♚c3 2 ♔d7 ♚c4 3 ♔c7 ♚c5 4 ♔b7 ♚d6 5 ♔xa7 ♚c7 *(D)*

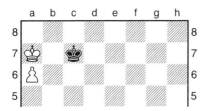

Both sides seem to have achieved their objectives and we have the same sort of position we saw on the last page. The white king cannot escape from the corner and the game is drawn.

Yes, but this did not have to happen!

In chess the shortest route between two points is not always a straight line!

The white king can go to a7 by either of the routes shown on the diagram. The diagonal journey appears longer but they both take five moves.

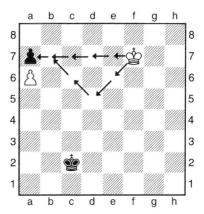

White could play **1 ♔e6! ♚c3 2 ♔d5!** and Black now has a problem. It isn't possible for his king to reach c7 in time because White's king is in the way. After **2...♚d3** (2...♚b4 3 ♔c6 ♚c4 is just the same) **3 ♔c6 ♚c4 4 ♔b7 ♚c5 5 ♔xa7 ♚c6** *(D)* he has lost a crucial move.

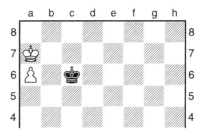

The black king hasn't got to c7 in time. It's White's move. He will play **6 ♔b8** and then promote his pawn.

You should remember the theory ... but always look for tricks in the specific position on the board.

21 The Square

Suppose it is Black's move in the position below. Can he catch the pawn before it promotes?

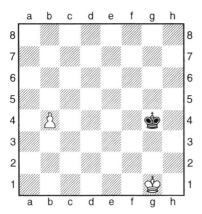

You might start analysing the position and say to yourself 'the king goes to f5 and the pawn to b5, the king goes to e6 and the pawn to b6, the king...'.

There has to be an easier way!

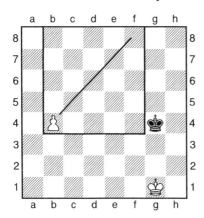

There is an easier way. You can use *the Square*.

A large square has been drawn on the last diagram. One side of the square goes from b4, where the pawn currently stands, to b8, where it wants to go. We call this the *pawn's square*.

There is a rule: *If the king can get inside the square, he will catch the pawn; if he can't, the pawn will promote safely.*

In the diagram position **1...\&f5** takes the king into the square. Now **2 b5 \&e6 3 b6 \&d6 4 b7 \&c7** *(D)* and Black has caught the pawn.

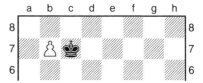

It can promote but it will be captured next move: **5 b8\&+ \&xb8**.

If it is White's turn to move in the original position he wins by **1 b5** *(D)*.

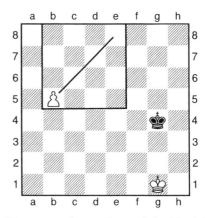

The square is smaller and the black king cannot get inside it: **1...\&f5 2 b6 \&e6 3 b7 \&d6** and the white pawn promotes safely: **4 b8\&+**.

Using the idea of the square will save you time and avoid the possibility of your making a mistake in calculation.

You still have to be careful though.

Black may have thought he was safe in this position:

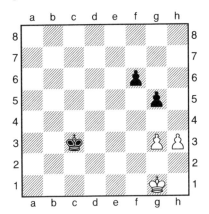

White can create a passed pawn on the h-file but the black king will be able to move inside its square:

1 h4 gxh4 2 gxh4 ♚d4 *(D)*

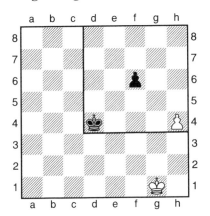

The king is inside the square but Black still has a problem. The king doesn't have a direct route to h8.

3 h5 ♚e5 4 h6

Now if Black didn't have the pawn on f6 he would play 4...♚f6 and catch the white pawn. However, the pawn is in the way. The black king has to go around it and this takes him out of the square.

4...♚e6 *(D)*

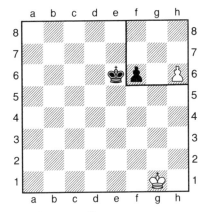

5 h7 ♚f7 6 h8♕ *(D)*

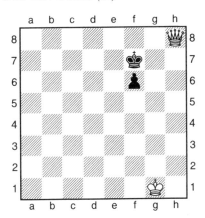

Black has lost a move and White has gained a queen!

You should use the idea of *the square* to help you but always check that there are no tricks in the position!

22 Counting in a Pawn Race

On the last page you saw how understanding *the square* made it easy to see whether a pawn could promote.

Counting is another little trick that can sometimes make life easier for yourself.

Look at the position below and see if you can work out the plans for both sides.

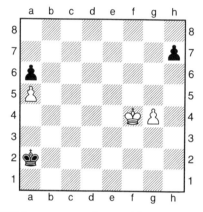

White wants to advance his king, grab the black h-pawn and then promote his own g-pawn.

Black wants to capture the white a-pawn with his king and then promote his own a-pawn.

Neither side's plan interferes with the other's. They can both carry out their plans independently.

So it will be a race! Who will win? Who will promote first?

Once again you can try analysing this, moving pieces around in your mind, but it is easier to *count*!

White's plan needs three king moves, to g5, h6 and capturing on h7. Then he needs four pawn moves, to g5, g6, g7 and finally g8. Three and four: a total of *seven* moves.

Black's plan requires four king moves, to a3 (or b3), a4 (or b4), capturing on a5 and then a further move to get off the a-file and out of the way of his own pawn. Then he needs five pawn moves, to a5, a4, a3, a2 and a1. Four and five: a total of *nine* moves.

Therefore White will win the race by two moves.

Even if it is Black's turn to move, White will win the race to promote the pawn. Let's see:

1...♔b3 2 ♔g5 ♔b4 3 ♔h6 ♔xa5 4 ♔xh7 ♔b4 5 g5 a5 6 g6 a4 7 g7 a3 8 g8♕ *(D)*

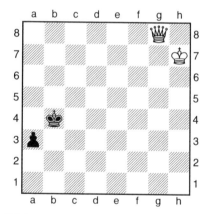

White has won the race in plenty of time to prevent Black from promoting his own pawn.

This was quite straightforward. The counting was easy since neither side had a choice of moves and White's winning margin was large.

Things can be more complicated!

Look at the position at the start of the next page and once again try to work out the plans for each side.

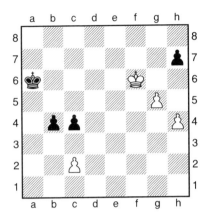

Black will advance on the b-file. It will take him *three moves* to promote his pawn: ...b3, ...b2 and ...b1♕. Of course after 1...b3 White can capture and Black will re-capture but these moves, one for each side, cancel each other out.

White has a choice of three plans:

a) He can use his king to capture the pawn on h7 and then promote his g-pawn. This will involve two king moves and three pawn moves: a total of *five moves*.

b) He can advance his pawn to g6, re-capture with the king after 1...hxg6 and then promote his h-pawn. This involves one move with the g-pawn and four with the h-pawn: a total of *five moves*. (We don't count the king's move because it was a re-capture and cancelled out Black's 1...hxg6.)

c) He can play h5 and then promote the g-pawn. This involves one move with the h-pawn and three with the g-pawn: a total of *four moves*. (Again we don't count an exchange of pawns on g6.)

So White's best plan will take four moves and Black's plan only three.

But whose turn is it to move?

Suppose it is Black's turn. He has a two-move advantage. One because his plan is quicker and one from moving first:

1...b3 2 cxb3 cxb3 3 h5 b2 4 g6 hxg6 5 hxg6 b1♕ 6 g7 (D)

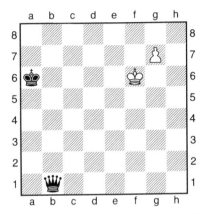

It is Black's move. He will play 6...♕b3 and prevent the g-pawn from promoting. Then he will approach the white pawn with his king and win it.

If it is White's turn to move in the original position Black has only the one-move advantage from his quicker plan:

1 h5 b3 2 cxb3 cxb3 3 g6 hxg6 4 hxg6 b2 5 g7 b1♕ and we have exactly the same position as in the diagram above with the important difference that it is White's turn to move and he will play **6 g8♕**.

Count carefully! Don't count a capture and recapture and make sure you know whose turn it is to move at the end of the calculation!

23 The Sting in the Tail

You have just seen how to count in a pawn race and you have seen that it is important to know whose turn it is to move at the end of the race. Now you have to go a step further and see if there is a *sting in the tail*.

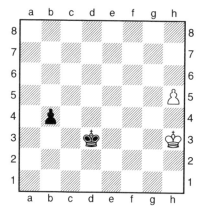

If you count in this position you will see that both sides need three moves to promote their pawns. It doesn't seem to matter whose turn it is to move because when one side promotes, the other will do the same immediately. Both sides will have king and queen and the game will be drawn. Right?

Wrong!

The moves **1 h6 b3 2 h7 b2 3 h8♕ b1♕** *(D)* take us to a position where both sides have promoted.

It is very easy in a game to work your way through a piece of calculation like this, come to a logical stopping point like this and end the thinking there with no more than a general judgement of the final position.

It would be very easy to look at the starting position above and concentrate our thoughts on the promotion of the pawns. We would reach the position in the diagram below and

might well think 'Both sides have got a queen and the position is equal'. This might well seem a logical point to stop thinking.

But we would be wrong!

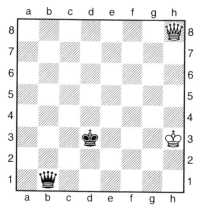

White can play **4 ♕h7+** *(D)*, the *sting in the tail*, and skewer king and queen.

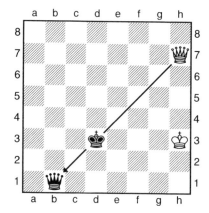

After Black's king escapes from check his queen is lost. Similarly, if it were Black's move in the top diagram he also has a winning skewer, 4...♕h1+.

At the end of any piece of analysis, you need to judge the position, but you also need to ask the important question *"What will happen next?"*

Furthermore, when you play over an *obvious* series of moves in your mind it is also easy to miss a better alternative along the way.

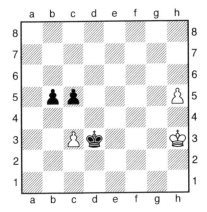

Here if Black plays 1...b4 2 cxb4 and recaptures with the *obvious* 2...cxb4 he will reach the position in the previous example and lose to the 6 ♕h7+ skewer.

But the *obvious* isn't always the *best*! After **1...b4 2 cxb4** Black can play **2...c4!** (D).

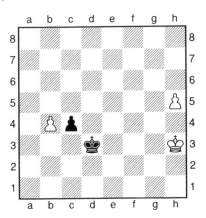

Then both sides will promote: **3 h6 c3 4 h7 c2 5 h8♕ c1♕** (D).

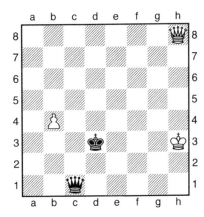

Now we can see the difference. The black queen is on c1 and not b1. 6 ♕h7+ is no longer a winning skewer – after 6...♔d4, Black keeps his queen and draws.

Try for Yourself 15

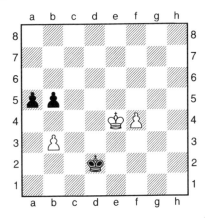

It is Black's turn to move. How should the game finish? You will need to count, to consider the square, to look for stings and think about the obvious!

(The solution is on page 60.)

24 King and Queen vs King and Pawn

Often a pawn race will end with one side promoting before the other, leaving a position like this, which we saw earlier on page 51.

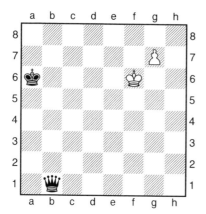

Winning here is straightforward for Black. He puts his queen on b3 and if necessary later on g8 and he patiently brings his king across the board and wins the white pawn.

But suppose the white king is on f8.

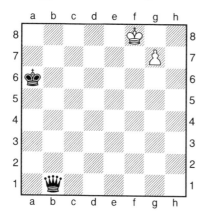

Now 1...♕b3? is no good because with the king's help White can safely promote his pawn.

You begin the winning method by driving the white king onto the g8-square, where it will block its own pawn. This is just one of several ways of doing so:

1...♕f5+ 2 ♔e8 ♕g6+ 3 ♔f8 ♕f6+ 4 ♔g8 *(D)*

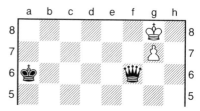

First step accomplished. The white king blocks its own pawn and this gives you the opportunity to move your king.

4...♔b6 *(D)*

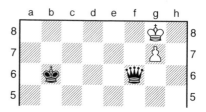

5 ♔h7

The white king pops its head out and is promptly pushed back in front of the pawn.

5...♕f7 6 ♔h8 ♕h5+ 7 ♔g8

This provides time for another king move:

7...♔c6 *(D)*

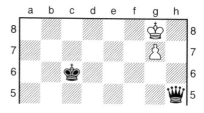

Winning is a slow process ... but it is sure and you just have to be patient.

8 ♔f8 ♛f5+ 9 ♔e8 ♛g6+ 10 ♔f8 ♛f6+ 11 ♔g8

Once again the white king is in front of its pawn, giving you the chance of another king move.

11...♚d7 (D)

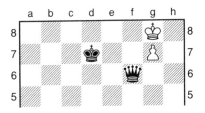

Black is gradually closing in.

12 ♔h7 ♛f7 13 ♔h8 ♛h5+ 14 ♔g8 (D)

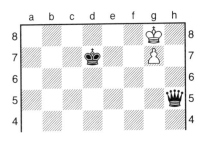

And what next? 14...♚e7 (D)?

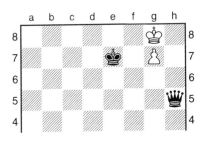

No!! Even in the simplest of positions things can go wrong and in the diagram above Black has managed to stalemate his opponent!

Apart from the fact that you should always be alert, the alarm bells should ring the moment you notice that White is gradually being squashed out of space.

The winning move for Black is **14...♚e6**, when White has to play **15 ♔f8** and is mated by **15...♛f7#** *(D)*.

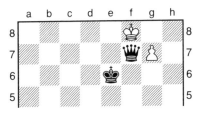

Try for Yourself 16

Set up the original position again and practise playing the position for yourself.

Then, before you turn over and read the next page, set up the position in the following diagram and see if you can still win for Black.

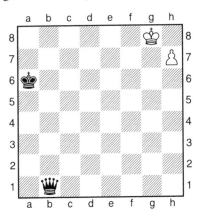

Try for Yourself 17

Now in the diagram above, move the pawn from h7 and put it on f7. Can Black win now? Does it matter which file the pawn stands on? You'll find out on the next page.

25 The h- and f-Pawn Exceptions

If the pawn stands on the h-file (or a-file) and it is supported by its king on the seventh or the eighth rank, the game will be drawn unless the enemy king is close enough to set up a checkmating position.

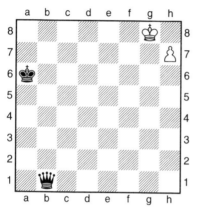

You will see the problem immediately if we continue with the winning method from the last page: **1...♕g6+ 2 ♔h8** (*D*).

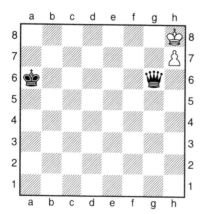

Remember that Black only has time to move his king across the board when the white king is in front of the pawn, preventing the pawn's advance.

In our position the white king *is* blocking the pawn so you would expect the black king to begin his travels with **2...♔b6** (*D*).

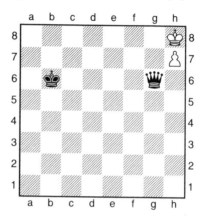

But if he does, it is stalemate! The white king has hit the edge of the board and cannot move.

Black can go on checking for ever but he will never have time to move his king. White only has to be careful that he doesn't fall asleep and get himself mated. **2...♕f6+ 3 ♔g8 ♕d8+ 4 ♔g7 ♕e7+ 5 ♔h8??** (he should play 5 ♔g8, when he is quite safe) **5...♕f8#** (*D*).

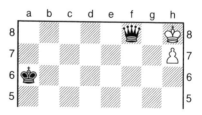

White has lost foolishly! As long as he keeps his king on the squares g7 and g8 and only goes to h8 when he is forced to do so, he has nothing to worry about.

There is a similar problem when the pawn is on the f-file (or c-file).

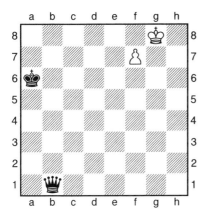

Black naturally begins with **1...♕g6+** and White, instead of replying with the obvious 2 ♔f8 which allows 2...♔b6, plays **2 ♔h8!** and if **2...♕xf7** *(D)* we have this position:

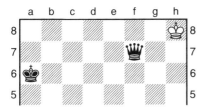

Stalemate! The white king has no move so the game is drawn.

The rules for king and queen against king and pawn are quite simple.

You will always stop the pawn from promoting unless it is on the seventh rank and supported by its own king.

When the pawn is on the seventh and when it is supported properly, you will only win if the pawn is on the b-, d-, e-, or g-file. You will have to be satisfied with a draw if

the pawn is on the a-, c-, f-, or h- file unless your king is already close enough for you to have mating ideas:

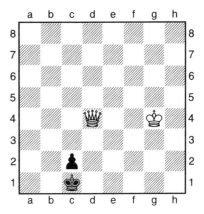

Here the black pawn will be allowed to promote: **1 ♕a1+ ♔d2 2 ♕b2 ♔d1 3 ♔f3!** and now **3...c1♕** allows **4 ♕e2#** *(D).*

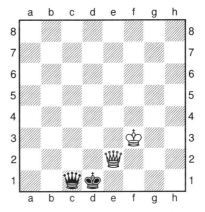

There are similar mating possibilities when an h- or a-pawn is on the seventh but only when the enemy king is close to the scene of action. Remember the general rule that rook's and bishop's pawn positions are drawn but remember also that as with all rules there will be exceptions!

26 The Breakthrough

A *breakthrough* is a simple device by which one pawn is sacrificed to allow another to break through and promote. It often arises in king and pawn endings. The following diagram provides an example.

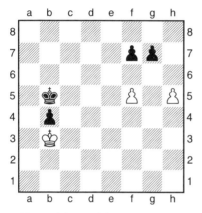

In this position White continues **1 f6!** *(D)* threatening 2 fxg7 followed by promotion. Yes, the pawn is *en prise*, but that's the whole point.

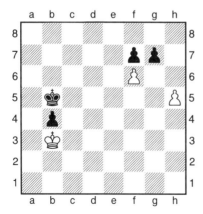

When Black takes the pawn with **1...gxf6** *(D)* he reaches the position in the next diagram.

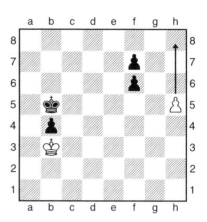

The white h-pawn has *broken through* the line of black defending pawns and he can run on and promote.

If you look back to the lower diagram in the previous column, you will see that Black had little choice. He can't ignore the f6-pawn and if instead of 1...gxf6 he plays 1...g6 or 1...g5 the white h-pawn is still free to promote.

The position in the next diagram occurred in a game in London in 1914.

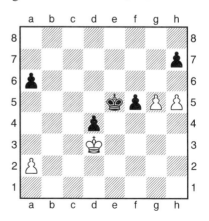

Presumably Edward Lasker, who was playing Black, didn't imagine he was in any danger of losing. However, José Raúl Capablanca spotted a *breakthrough*.

Capablanca *did not* continue 1 g6?. This *breakthrough* does not work due to 1...hxg6 2 h6 ♚f6 *(D)*, when the black king is inside the pawn's *square*.

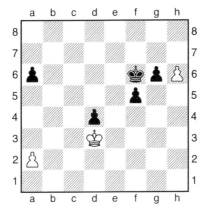

No, in the original position Capablanca played **1 h6!** *(D)*.

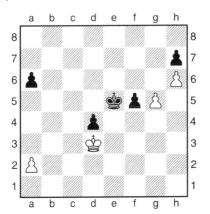

The *breakthrough* 2 g6 is threatened and Black has no good move. Lasker cannot prevent 2 g6 and he cannot get his king back to the corner in time:

1...♚e6 2 g6! ♚f6 (or 2...hxg6 3 h7 and the pawn promotes) **3 gxh7** *(D)*.

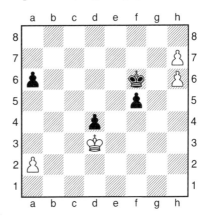

Black's king can't move inside the *square* of the h7-pawn since g7 is covered by the h6-pawn. Therefore the h7-pawn will inevitably promote.

A line of defensive pawns may seem to be a barrier but you must be alert to a sacrifice deflecting one of the defenders.

Try for Yourself 18

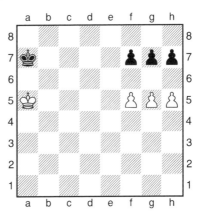

How does White break through in this position?

(The solution is on page 60.)

Try for Yourself Solutions

13)

a) 1...♚f6? allows the white king a clear run: 2 ♚d5 (or 2 ♚c5) 2...♚e7 3 ♚c6, etc.

b) 1...♚f7? also allows the king through by 2 ♚d5 or 2 ♚c5, but not by 2 ♚e5?, when 2...♚e7 hands Black the opposition and White is foiled.

c) 1...♚e7? allows 2 ♚c5. White could also play 2 ♚e5, when he has the opposition, but not 2 ♚d5?, which allows Black to block him with 2...♚d7.

d) After 1...♚d7? White must play 2 ♚d5! since both 2 ♚e5? ♚e7 and 2 ♚c5? ♚c7 leave Black with the opposition.

e) 1...♚d6! is correct, when Black has the opposition and White cannot make progress.

14)

1 ♚c2 ♚e7 2 ♚b3 ♚d6 and now in order to win White must take his king on a journey around the pawn: **3 ♚a4!** (note that 3 ♚c4? would not win because Black can play 3...♚c6 and gain the opposition himself) **3...♚c6 4 ♚a5 ♚b7** (or 4...♚c7 5 ♚a6!) **5 ♚b5**. White has his king in front of his pawn and has gained the opposition.

15)

White already has a passed pawn and Black will gain one with **1...a4**. Black's king cannot get within White's *square*. White's king could go to d4 to get into Black's *square* but he can't cross c3 so he can't catch the pawn. Counting tells us that White needs four moves to promote his pawn, and Black three. As it is now White to move it looks as though both pawns can queen at the same time.

If we continue with the *obvious* moves that is just what happens: 2 bxa4 bxa4 3 f5 a3 4 f6 a2 5 f7 a1♛ 6 f8♛. Is there a *sting in the tail*? No, Black cannot win White's queen. But that of course is playing the obvious moves and after **2 bxa4** Black has the better option **2...b4** because **3 f5 b3 4 f6 b2 5 f7 b1♛+** is *check*! By promoting on b1 instead of a1 there is a *sting in the tail*. White does not have time to promote his pawn – he has to move his king and Black will play **6...♛b4**.

Notice that it makes no difference if White plays 3 a5 and tries to promote his a-pawn. Black will still queen with check and then play 6...♛a1.

18)

The classic *breakthrough* position!

White plays **1 g6!**. Black must capture and it doesn't matter which way. A white pawn *breaks through* after both **1...fxg6 2 h6! gxh6 3 f6** and after **1...hxg6 2 f6! gxf6 3 h6**.

4 Opening Principles

The opening is a most important stage of the game because it is in the opening that you will begin to place your forces for the battle that lies ahead and it is in the opening that you will begin to make your plans. Good opening play can set you on the road to victory whereas bad opening play can quickly lead to disaster.

There are many different openings for White and defences for Black, and they range from very sound to extremely risky. What you choose to play will be according to your style and your temperament.

Look at the bookstall at any chess congress and you will find countless books written on every one of these countless openings. You will find countless (well, upwards of ten thousand) moves in each book. What should you learn? What should you know?

You should learn the basic principles of opening play as they are explained on the next few pages here and then learn the basic ideas behind the openings and defences you intend to play. Don't spend too much time memorizing moves and variations. If you understand the principles you will be able to work out many of the basic moves for yourself.

27 Development

Can you see why Black lost the following game?

1 e4 e5 2 d4 exd4 3 c3 dxc3 4 ♗c4 cxb2 5 ♗xb2 ♛g5 *(D)*

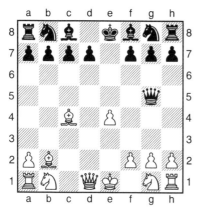

6 ♘f3 ♛xg2? 7 ♗xf7+ ♚d8 *(D)*

Black dare not capture the bishop since 7...♚xf7 8 ♖g1 ♛h3? 9 ♘g5+ forks his king and queen.

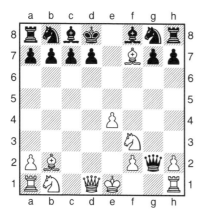

8 ♖g1 ♗b4+ 9 ♘c3 ♛h3 10 ♖g3 ♛h6 11 ♛b3 *(D)*

White is threatening to win a piece. He threatens both 12 ♛xb4 and 12 ♗xg8.

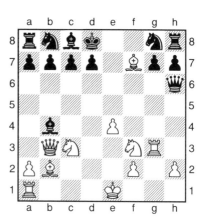

11...♗xc3+ 12 ♛xc3 ♘f6 13 ♖g6! *(D)*

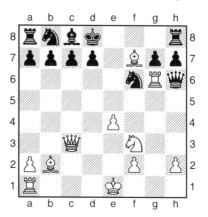

An amazing move! The point is that the black queen will be cut off from the defence of f6.

13...hxg6

Black could have avoided mate if he had played 13...♘xe4 14 ♖xh6 ♘xc3 15 ♗xc3 ♖f8 but White's massive attack is still winning after 16 ♘g5. Likewise 13...♛xg6 14 ♗xg6 hxg6 15 ♘g5 offers no real defensive chances for Black.

14 ♛xf6+ gxf6 15 ♗xf6# *(D)*

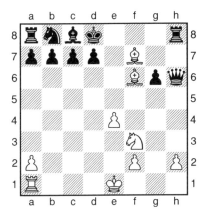

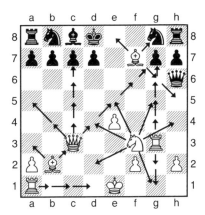

Paris in 1879 was the scene of this glorious massacre. Schnitzler (White) was the winner and Alexandre (Black) his unfortunate victim.

To understand why Black lost, we need to look back at the final position of the game shown in the above diagram.

Black has a queen, a rook and a pawn for a bishop – certainly a big material advantage!

But what can Black's pieces do? And what have they actually done during the game?

Very little!

Four of Black's five pieces never moved in the whole game. Two of them cannot move even now.

All of White's pieces took part in his attack except the a1-rook, which was always ready to leap into action if needed.

Let's look again at the position after White's twelfth move.

White's pieces are *developed*. They are at battle stations, ready for action. They all have many squares to which they can move.

Of Black's pieces, only his queen is *developed*. All of his other pieces are stuck on their home squares. They aren't ready to attack and they aren't even in a position to defend.

Black lost because his *undeveloped* pieces could not help him when White threw his whole *developed* army into the attack.

Your first job in a game of chess is to *develop* your pieces.

You need to bring each piece out and put it on a square where it will be safe and where it will be well placed when you need it to attack or to defend.

Development will become a race. If you win the race, your pieces will be first into action and you will be ready to meet anything your opponent may throw at you!

28 The Importance of Time

You are on your marks.
'Set!'.
The starter raises his pistol and fires.
You sit up in the blocks.
You yawn.
You stretch.
You slowly stagger to your feet.
Will you win this race?
Of course not!
In a race you can't afford to waste time.
Development is a race.
A chess race.
You cannot afford to lose time in that race or your opponent will have his pieces *developed* before you are ready.

There are five simple rules of *development*.
Four *don'ts* and one *do*.
Alexandre ignored three of the *don'ts* in his game on the previous page.

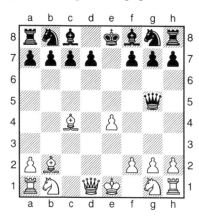

Alexandre has just played 5...♕g5? and he intends to play 6...♕xg2. Definitely a bad idea!
Why?

The first don't: Don't go out of your way to pinch pawns in the opening. You will only waste time.
The second don't: Don't move the same piece more than once unless you have to do so. You will only waste time.
The third don't: Don't begin to attack until you have most of your pieces developed. You will only be beaten back and waste time.
Schnitzler countered Black's bad plan with the *do*.
The do: Develop aggressively if you can. If you can develop a piece with a threat you may gain time.
We can see how this all works if we play on a few moves.
5...♕g5 begins to attack before the other pieces are developed and the queen will be going out of her way, wasting time pinching the g2-pawn.
6 ♘f3 is aggressive development: it brings a piece into play and gains time by attacking the queen.
6...♕xg2 begins the 'attack', it pinches a pawn and it moves the queen a second time.
After **7 ♗xf7+ ♔d8, 8 ♖g1** is another piece of aggressive development, putting the rook on a good file and gaining time by attacking the queen.
After **8...♗b4+ 9 ♘c3, 9...♕h3** (D) is forced but this third move with the queen means Black has lost even more time.
The result is the position in the next diagram. Compare this with the diagram on the left and you will see that White has simply gained the two good developing moves ♘f3 and ♖g1 whilst the black queen is no better on h3 than she was on g5.

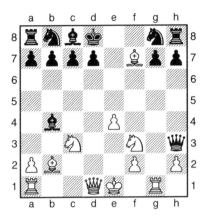

Finally, *the fourth don't*. Don't make pawn moves unless they help your development. Pawn moves are not developing moves. They are only useful if they help you to develop a piece or if they support a piece when it is developed.

In the position below White began by moving his pawn to e4.

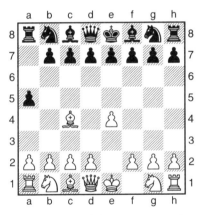

This was a useful pawn move in two ways.

Firstly, it opened the diagonals for his queen and bishop and enabled him to play the move ♗c4.

Secondly, on e4 the pawn supports the bishop. It attacks d5 and prevents Black from playing ...d5, which would otherwise drive the bishop away.

Black's ...a5 was a poor pawn move. It does not help his development since he loses rook for bishop if he plays ...♖a6 and it won't help support any other piece.

Don't attack before you have developed your pieces.

Don't go out of your way to pinch pawns in the opening.

Don't move pieces more than once in the opening unless you are forced to do so.

Don't make unnecessary pawn moves.

Do try to develop aggressively.

Try for Yourself 19

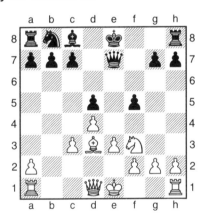

Four moves are suggested for Black in this position. Which would you play?

a)   1...♕a3

b)   1...f4

c)   1...0-0

d)   1...g5

(The answer is on page 74.)

29 Pieces and the Centre

Pieces placed in or towards the centre of the board will be more powerful than those on the edge.

Let's compare the power of the knights in the diagram below. How many squares does each attack or control?

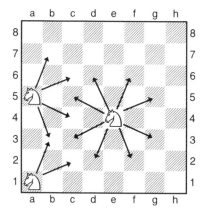

The central knight on e4 commands eight squares.

The a5-knight attacks half that number, just four squares.

The a1-knight can move to only two squares.

This difference in strength is most marked with the knight, but it affects all the other pieces to some extent, with the exception of the rook.

Because it is powerfully placed in the centre, the e4-knight can move rapidly in any direction. It can reach any edge of the board in just two moves.

Both the a1- and a5-knights will take twice as long, four moves, to trundle over to the opposite side of the board.

The next position shows why this is important.

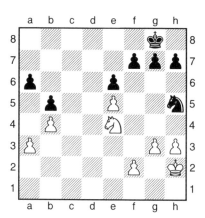

In the centre, the powerful white knight hits in all directions.

If it is his move, White has the simple plan of ♘c5, ♘xa6, ♘c7 and ♘xb5, winning easily.

The black king and knight are far too slow to come to the rescue of the pawns. However, if the black knight were centrally placed, for example on d5, it would just drop back to c7 when White played ♘c5 and Black would be safe.

Let's put some more pieces on the board.

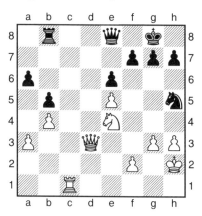

All three of White's pieces are either in the centre or attack the centre. This allows them to have a great choice of moves and gives White plenty of possible plans:

His knight can go to g5 where it supports the queen's attack on h7 and also hits the f7-pawn.

The knight can go to d6 to attack the black queen and to hit f7.

The knight can go to c5 and attack the a6-pawn.

White's queen is already in action along the d-file. She can invade deeper into Black's territory on d6 or she can switch to f3, to attack the black knight, or to another square along the third rank.

His rook can crash into Black's position on c7 and attack f7 or it can switch to d1 and support its queen.

And what can the black pieces do?

Very little!

The game Walker-Hill, Oxford 1964 ended quickly: **1 ♖c7 ♖d8 2 ♘d6 f6 3 ♕b3 ♕g6 4 ♕xe6+ ♔h8** (or 4...♔f8 5 ♕e7+ ♔g8 6 ♕xd8+) **5 ♘f7+ ♔g8 6 ♘xd8+** *(D)* and Black resigned.

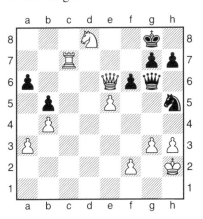

Their beautiful central positions gave all the power to the white pieces and they smashed Black's defences apart. But the centre is not all about attacking.

Pieces centrally placed are also likely to be good defenders.

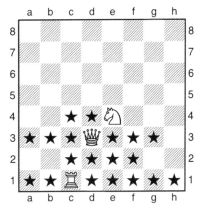

Even if Black's pieces were better placed, they would have great difficulty invading White's position because every one of the squares marked with a star in the diagram is defended by at least one of White's three pieces. (The squares g2, h3, h4, g4 and f4 are protected by White's king and pawns.)

By contrast, White's rook was able to invade on c7 and his knight on d6 (or c5) as Black's pieces had no control over those squares.

You must remember the importance of the centre when you develop your pieces in the opening.

You will not be able to place all of your pieces in the middle of the board straight away. You and your opponent will be fighting to control the central squares, but you should develop your pieces towards the centre and be ready to occupy a central square when the opportunity arises.

30 Pawns and the Centre

Pawns placed in the centre of the board give several advantages. If White could have two moves instead of one with his first go, he might well play 1 e4 and 2 d4.

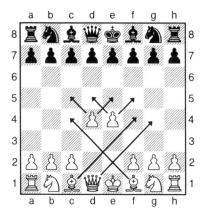

a) The moves 1 e4 and 2 d4 have opened lines for White's queen and bishops to develop.

(Note that if instead of occupying the two central squares, the pawns had just advanced one square each, to e3 and to d3, they would be blocking the diagonals of the bishops.)

b) The pawns attack the four squares c5, d5, e5 and f5 and prevent Black from developing pieces on any of those squares.

c) The pawns make it more difficult for Black to put a pawn in the centre. White can now play 3 ♗c4 or 3 ♗f4 without having to worry about Black immediately playing ...d5 or ...e5.

Pawns in the centre can also help to create useful space for your pieces and cramp your opponent. We saw this with this pawn-structure on the last page:

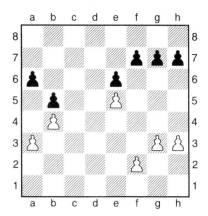

White controls more space because his e-pawn is two squares further up the board than Black's e-pawn.

On e5, the pawn provided wonderful cover for the e4-square, which White used as a base for his knight. It cramped Black, preventing him from putting a piece on d6 or f6. It prevented Black from advancing his own e-pawn. (How Black would have loved to have been able to play ...e5 and ...♕e6, opening up his position and getting more room for his pieces.)

White used the great area of space in the centre to manoeuvre his pieces into attacking positions.

At the beginning of the game you should aim to put at least one pawn on a square where it attacks the centre – and you should aim to keep it there!

31 Castling and the Centre

Castling serves two purposes.

First you are looking after your king. When you advance your e-pawn or your d-pawn you may be opening lines for your bishops but you are also opening lines for your opponent's pieces to get at your king. The longer your king is stuck in the centre the more likely he is to be attacked.

When you castle, you put your king into a safer position behind a protective shield of pawns.

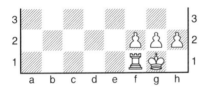

Second, you are developing your rooks. Rooks need open files.

Open files appear where pawns are exchanged.

In the opening, pawns are most likely to be exchanged in the centre.

Castling brings a rook towards the centre.

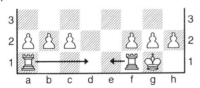

Rooks can work very well as a pair, either side by side or doubled on the same file. Castling gets the king out of the way and brings the rooks together.

In most games you will castle on the kingside. Usually the kingside pieces are developed first and usually the king will be safer on the kingside.

However, you can also castle queenside:

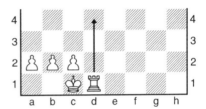

This seems to save a move because the rook is developed straight onto the d-file. When you castle kingside your rook ends up on f1 and will probably have to move again.

But the move gained will be lost if you have to play ⌘b1 later on. Your king will be tucked away safer on b1 and he may also be needed to defend the a2-pawn.

In general you should try to castle early.
Put your king into safety.
Bring your rooks to the centre.

32 Gambits

A *gambit* is an opening in which one player gives up material in the hope of gaining an advantage in position.

We saw the moves **1 e4 e5 2 d4 exd4 3 c3 dxc3 4 ♗c4 cxb2 5 ♗xb2** *(D)* in the game Schnitzler vs Alexandre.

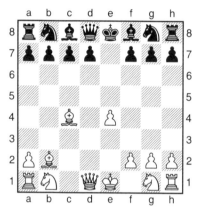

The moves 1 e4 e5 2 d4 exd4 3 c3 are known as the Danish Gambit.

White's advantages are obvious.

White has a lead in development.

White has open files and diagonals, plenty of space for his pieces to use.

White has a solid pawn in the centre.

White has got rid of Black's central pawn.

Black's advantage is also obvious: he has two extra pawns!

Over a hundred years ago it was considered almost a matter of honour to accept a gambit and to try to hang on to the material. The world's greatest players used gambit openings and created some wonderful attacking games. This King's Gambit was played between McDonnell and Tyssen in London in 1834:

1 e4 e5 2 f4 exf4 3 ♘f3 g5 4 ♗c4 g4 5 ♘c3 gxf3 6 0-0 fxg2? 7 ♖xf4 *(D)*

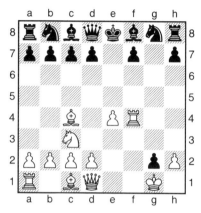

A typically wild gambit position.

White has an advantage in space and development. Black has a knight and a pawn.

Black now blundered horribly. Trying to prevent 8 ♗xf7+, he played **7...f6??**, allowing **8 ♕h5+ ♔e7 9 ♕f7+ ♔d6 10 e5+ ♔xe5 11 ♖e4+** *(D)* and Black resigned.

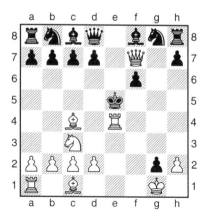

The Golden Age of the Gambits passed as players developed better defensive techniques. In the next game, a King's Bishop's

Gambit, Paul Morphy demonstrated one method as Black against Budzinsky in Paris in 1859:

1 e4 e5 2 f4 exf4 3 ♗c4 d5 *(D)*

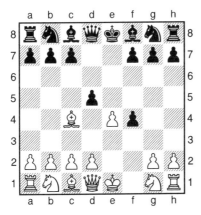

Having 'won' a pawn, Morphy promptly gives it back in order to open lines for his queen and bishop and make sure that he doesn't fall behind in development.

4 ♗xd5 ♘f6 5 ♘c3 ♗b4 6 d3? ♘xd5 7 exd5 0-0 8 ♕f3 ♖e8+ 9 ♘e2 ♗xc3+ 10 bxc3 ♕h4+ 11 g3? ♗g4 *(D)*

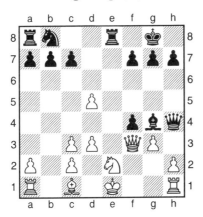

White resigned since the knight on e2 is lost. At no stage in the game was Morphy behind in development.

Nowadays the classical gambit openings are far less common in grandmaster play. Most gambits are played by White and the modern grandmaster prefers more reliable methods of using the advantage of having the first move. The Queen's Gambit, **1 d4 d5 2 c4**, is one of White's most popular options, but this is not a true gambit. If **2...dxc4** White can, if he wishes, make sure of regaining the pawn by **3 e3** *(D)*, intending a quick ♗xc4. Any attempts by Black to cling onto the c4-pawn are then very dubious.

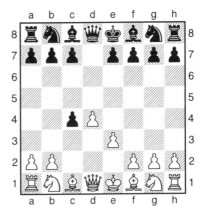

Although modern grandmasters are willing to take risks and sacrifice material, they generally prefer to obtain more subtle positional compensation than the temporary lead in development granted by the old-fashioned swashbuckling gambit openings.

Should you play speculative gambit openings? A good question. Turn to the next page before you decide!

33 Choosing Your Openings

Different openings lead to different sorts of game. What sort of game do you like?

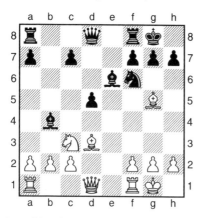

A position from a *Scotch Game*. Both sides have good development and there is plenty of space for all the pieces. The rooks can easily come into play onto the d- and e-files for White, and the e- and b-files for Black.

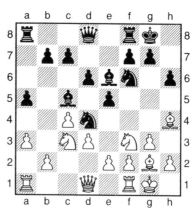

Here we see a line of the *English Opening*. Both sides have their knights and bishops in action but there are no open lines for the rooks. The two players will have to decide when and how to advance pawns and open up the position.

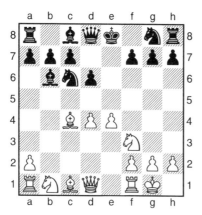

This position is from the *Evans Gambit*. White has a lead in development and much more space, but in compensation Black has an extra pawn. His position is cramped but solid.

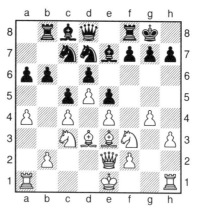

A completely blocked centre from a *Czech Benoni*. Black is getting ready to advance his pawns on the queenside, starting with ...b5. White is preparing to attack on the kingside.

Which of the four games would you prefer to play, and would you rather be Black or White?

You are not Garry Kasparov. You do not have Kasparov's arms and legs, you do not have his face and you do not have his brain. You are not him.

You are *you*!

You are an individual. Your brain, your physical strength and your emotions are unique to you. There is nobody else in this world quite like you.

Maybe one day, like Vladimir Kramnik, you will beat Garry Kasparov. Maybe one day you will be better than him. Maybe one day you will be the world's number one!

Wow! But why not?

However, if you are to achieve fame it will be because you will have recognized *your* strengths and you will have played to them.

Study the play of the great players both modern and old. Listen to your teachers or advisers. Watch your clubmates. But remember, you are *you*! What is good for others will not necessarily be right for you.

Many school, club and tournament players use all the wrong reasons for choosing the openings they play. Perhaps they copy Kasparov or another favourite player.

Perhaps they dream of playing a beautiful sacrificial game and play the Danish Gambit like Schnitzler.

Perhaps they follow fashion and play what is popular in master chess at the time.

One international master confided to me that as a junior he played the Philidor Defence simply because he liked the sound of the name.

Don't play openings for the wrong reasons – play them for the right reasons!

Understand that different openings lead to different sorts of game. That is obvious from the four positions opposite.

You have to decide which sort of game best suits you – and that's all down to you, your nature and your emotions.

Are you happy taking risks?

Are you happy to defend and to look for the chance to counter-attack or do you always feel the need to be doing something aggressive yourself?

Can you calculate calmly in the middle of complicated combinations?

Are you impatient?

Do you enjoy slow manoeuvring or are you easily bored if nothing exciting is happening?

It is not easy analysing yourself and working out your own chess style but it is easy deciding which openings will suit you ... especially if you have a chess computer against which you can match your ideas.

To find out whether an opening will suit you, begin by setting up a position after ten moves or so, rather as we have done opposite.

Now begin analysing.

Do ideas come easily to you? Can you find lots of plans to choose from? Does the position seem interesting? Are you excited by what seems likely to happen? Can you see things the opponent might do? Do his plans worry you?

Now play just three or four moves against the computer.

Did things work out as you expected? Did you feel happy and confident? Have you ended up in a position you like?

Repeat this process from the same position and from other positions in the same opening.

You will soon learn whether you have a feel for the opening.

Next, try the opening out in a real game. Don't worry too much about the result. It is more important how the game went, how you felt playing it. If you lost, you can always find out the reason why, and correct the mistake next time.

Remember: an opening is a bit like a set of clothes. If they feel right, they are right! If you feel comfortable in a game then the opening was a good one for you.

Finally, remember that it is more important to learn the ideas and plans associated with an opening than to learn by heart lots of moves and variations.

Try for Yourself Solution

19)

a) 1...♕a3, attacking the c3-pawn, is a poor idea because it wastes time moving the queen again. White may defend the pawn with the aggressive developing move 2 ♕c2, hitting the f5-pawn, or he may just ignore the threat and play 2 0-0, tempting Black to waste more time with 2...♕xc3, a third queen move.

b) 1...f4 is also a bad idea because Black is beginning an attack before he is fully developed. The game might continue 2 0-0 fxe3 3 fxe3 ♕xe3+ 4 ♔h1 0-0 5 ♕c2 with ♖ae1 to follow. White has a massive lead in development and consequently a massive attack.

c) 1...0-0 is best. It is a sound developing move putting the king into safety and bringing the rook into play.

d) 1...g5 is a 'nothing' pawn move. It supports the idea of a black attack with ...f4 but it does not help Black's development in any way. White might simply play 2 0-0 and extend his lead in development or open the attacking line for his queen to h5 with 2 ♘e5.

5 The Power of the Pieces

Your pieces are your strength, your main fighting force. How strong they are and how much of a fighting force they make will depend upon where you place them on the board. Each of your pieces has its own particular way of moving and each will require its own particular conditions so that it can be most effective.

   You should always be on the lookout for good squares for your pieces and for moves that will make them stronger. But you should never forget that throughout the game the position changes. A piece which is powerful one moment may become useless when a pawn is moved or exchanged, or another piece becomes dominant. You should spend time, particularly when it is your opponent's turn to move, to study the position in detail, to look at each of your pieces and to see how it might be made more useful. Similarly, you should look to weaken the power of the enemy pieces.

34 The Value of the Pieces

The pieces in a chess game have two values. The first is what we will call their *value in the bank*.

$\unicode{x2659}$ = 1
$\unicode{x2658}$ = 3
$\unicode{x2657}$ = 3 (or 3¼)
$\unicode{x2656}$ = 5
$\unicode{x2655}$ = 9 (or 9½)

Adding up the value of the pieces will always give you some idea of who may be winning a game, especially as you reach the endgame. But this figure is only their *bank value*.

Pieces have a second value, their *practical value*.

A tank is a useful weapon of war. It's fast, it's manoeuvrable and its turret can rotate through a full 360 degrees to hurl a massive shell hundreds of yards in any direction. In the middle of a large open battlefield the tank is mighty powerful!

But what about in the thick of a forest? Or in the narrow side-street of a town with the road blocked ahead, walls either side and no room to swivel the turret?

The tank has its *bank value*, what it cost, what it's worth, and it also has its *practical value*, what use it is, what it can actually do at any given time.

The *practical value* of your chess pieces will depend upon where they stand on the board and upon the power of other pieces around them.

The *bank value* of the pieces suggests that this position from a game in a Russian junior tournament is equal.

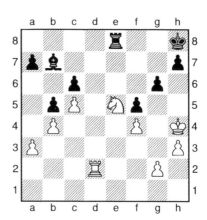

The position isn't equal because the *practical value* of the pieces is enormously to White's advantage.

White's knight is powerfully placed. It has a marvellous central position firing in all directions and in particular hitting the c6-pawn.

In comparison, Black's bishop is a miserable creature. It is blocked by its own pawns, it has only three possible moves (each only one square long!) and it is tied to defending the wretched c6-pawn.

White's rook is immensely powerful on the open d-file, threatening to invade on d6, d7 or, given the chance, d8.

The black rook seems to have plenty of space but what can he do and where can he go? What use is he?

Even the white king is more powerful than Black's! He threatens to march straight into Black's camp.

The game finished spectacularly:

1 $\unicode{x2656}$d7 $\unicode{x2657}$a8 2 $\unicode{x2654}$g5

White has several ways of winning. Obviously 2 $\unicode{x2656}$xa7 is also good.

2...♔g8 3 ♔h6 ♖c8

White was threatening 4 ♖g7+, when 4...♔h8 5 ♘f7# and 4...♔f8 5 ♘d7# are both mate.

4 ♖g7+ ♔f8 5 ♘d7+ ♔e8 6 ♘f6+ *(D)*

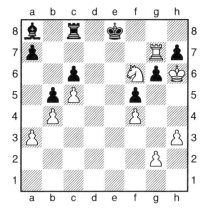

The *bank value* of the pieces remains equal ... but what about the *practical value*?

The *practical value* of Black's pieces is even less than it was six moves ago. His bishop has been shunted into a corner and his rook kicked sideways to a useless file. On the other hand, the *practical value* of White's army has increased. White's pieces have taken up more forward and aggressive positions and they are working well together. Notice how the rook and knight combine to deliver mate after 6...♔d8 7 ♖d7#.

6...♔f8 7 ♔xh7 ♖d8 8 ♔xg6 ♖d2

At last the black rook has some *practical value*. It has found something to do – it's attacking the g2-pawn – but it's all too late.

9 ♖f7# *(D)*

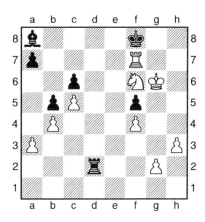

The problem you have to tackle in a game is balancing the *bank* and *practical values* of the pieces. In the Danish Gambit, after 1 e4 e5 2 d4 exd4 3 c3 dxc3 4 ♗c4 cxb2 5 ♗xb2 the *bank value* of Black's pieces is two points greater but the immediate *practical value* of White's pieces is much higher. In simple terms this means that White has to achieve something with his better-placed pieces or Black's points in the *bank* will win in the long run.

It is important that you keep the *bank value* of the pieces in your mind. This table may help you when exchanging, but remember that even the bank values are only approximate. Note in particular that in the middlegame two minor pieces are almost always better than rook + pawn.

♘ = ♗ = ♙♙♙
♖ = ♗♙♙ = ♘♙♙
♗♘ = ♖♙
♕ = ♖♗♙ = ♗♗♘
♖♖ = ♕♙

35 Open Lines

Your pieces are stronger when they stand on open lines.

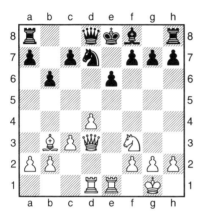

White has a lead in development but the lines of his queen, his rooks and his bishop are blocked either by his own d-pawn or Black's e6-pawn.

Lines become open when pawns are exchanged, so...

1 d5! *(D)*

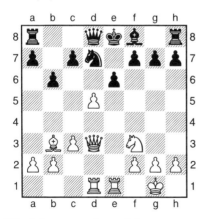

Black has several possible moves.

a) **1...♘c5 2 ♕b5+ ♕d7 3 dxe6! ♕xb5 4 exf7#** *(D)*.

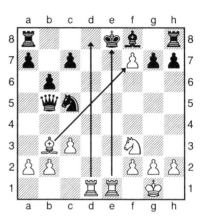

Open lines lead to mate! White's rooks power down the centre. His bishop supports at long range while the pawn actually delivers mate.

b) **1...♗e7 2 dxe6 fxe6 3 ♗xe6 ♘c5 4 ♕b5+** *(D)* and Black loses his queen.

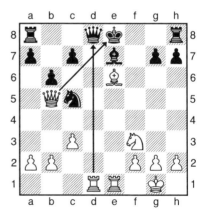

After the exchange of pawns White's pieces have exploded into action.

c) **1...♗d6 2 dxe6 fxe6 3 ♖xe6+ ♔f8 4 ♕d5** (threatening 5 ♖xd6 and 6 ♕f7#)

4...♘f6 5 ♖xf6+ ♕xf6 6 ♕xa8+ ♔e7 7 ♖e1+ ♔d7 8 ♗a4+ *(D).*

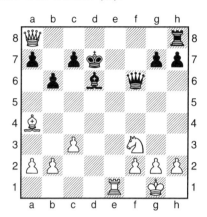

All the white pieces have lovely open lines and mate is inevitable: **8...c6 9 ♕xc6+ ♔d8 10 ♕d7#**.

d) **1...e5** *(D).*

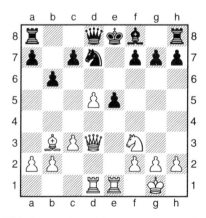

This leaves the white pawn on d5 blocking the d-file and the bishop on b3 but it still doesn't do Black any good!

2 ♘xe5 ♘xe5

If 2...♗e7, the reply 3 ♘c6 is murderous.

3 ♗a4+ ♔e7

3...♕d7 costs Black his queen.

4 ♖xe5+ ♔d6 5 ♖ee1 *(D)*

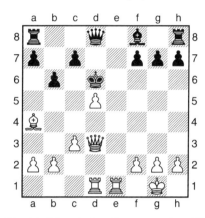

Black's king is fatally exposed to White's active pieces. Mate is inevitable again; e.g.: 5...♕g5 6 ♕b5 and ♕c6#.

Try for Yourself 20

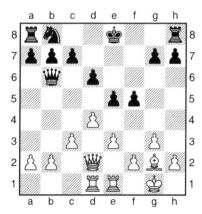

If it is White's move, should he play 1 d5 or 1 dxe5? And suppose it is Black's move. What should he do?

(The answer is on page 93.)

36 The Back Rank and the Pawn-Shield

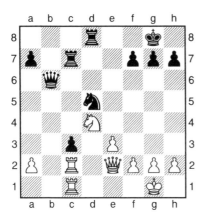

Ossip Bernstein surveyed this position in his game with José Raúl Capablanca in Moscow in 1914 and decided that the nasty black pawn on c3 just had to go.

Bernstein forked rook and pawn with **1 ♘b5** and after **1...♖c5** he removed the offending foot-soldier with **2 ♘xc3**. He had considered the exchanges **2...♘xc3 3 ♖xc3 ♖xc3 4 ♖xc3** *(D)*.

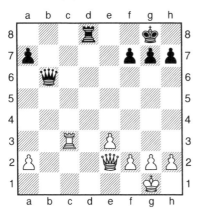

Here he expected 4...♕b1+ 5 ♕f1. He had cleverly foreseen that Capablanca would have to play 5...♕xa2 since the obvious 5...♖d1

would lose to 6 ♖c8+ *(D)* and mate on the eighth rank (or *back rank*).

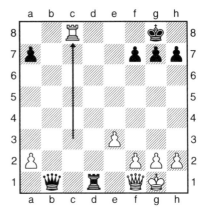

Sadly for Bernstein, he was thinking about the wrong back rank! Capablanca stunned him with **4...♕b2!!** *(D)*.

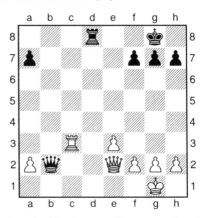

Yes, the black queen is *en prise* but Bernstein's queen is needed to defend *his own* back rank. 5 ♕xb2 ♖d1# is mate. As 5 ♖c2 ♕b1+ 6 ♕f1 ♕xc2, 5 ♕e1 ♕xc3 6 ♕xc3 ♖d1+ and 5 ♕c2 ♕a1+ 6 ♕c1 ♖d1+ are all equally horrible, Bernstein decided to resign.

At some time or other every beginner lives through two nightmares. One is when a knight descends seemingly unnoticed out of a clear blue sky to deliver a murderous fork. The other is when a rook skips the length of the board to embarrass the king on his back rank.

The warning bells should be ringing at the back of your mind as long as the pawns are unmoved in front of the king.

The ringing should become louder if the pieces leave the back rank unprotected.

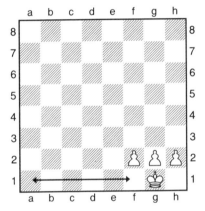

However, do not be tempted to waste a move early in the game by advancing one of the pawns in the king's defensive shield just to avoid the possibility of a back-rank mate twenty moves later!

The king will usually be safer from a frontal attack with his pawns in line as they are in the diagram above. Only play a move such as g3 or h3 if it becomes really necessary.

Try for Yourself 21

Even if a pawn has advanced in front of the king you still have to think about the back rank, especially if an enemy bishop is aimed at the king's escape square. Mikhail Tal forgot this in his game with Fridrik Olafsson in Moscow 1971.

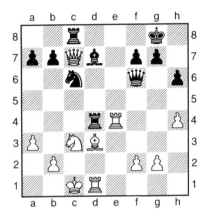

Tal has just played ...♖c8 to attack the white queen. Can you see why this move was a mistake?

Try for Yourself 22

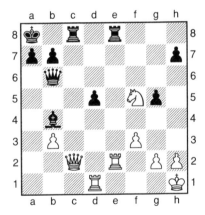

This position arose in the Teschner vs Portisch game at Monaco in 1969. The position of the pieces on the c- and e-files is interesting but it was the d-file that attracted Teschner's attention.

Can White safely play 1 ♖xd5?

(The solutions are on page 93.)

37 Rooks and the Seventh Rank

A rook on the seventh rank can be very well placed, sniping at enemy pawns and setting up tactical possibilities.

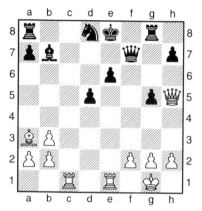

At Dresden in 1969 Hübner was a piece up. No doubt he was confident until Antunac played **1 ♖c7!**, leaving his queen *en prise*. The game continued **1...♕xh5 2 ♖e7+ ♔f8** *(D)*.

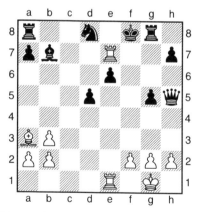

The rook and bishop form a perfect partnership and White can play 3 ♖xh7+ and regain his queen, although this would still leave him a piece down.

But what's the hurry? The queen isn't going anywhere!

First of all Antunac collected a bishop with **3 ♖xb7+ ♔e8** and then the black queen with **4 ♖e7+ ♔f8 5 ♖xh7+** *(D)*.

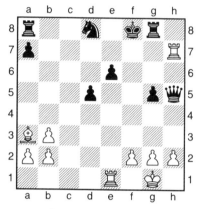

Now **5...♔e8 6 ♖xh5** left him two pawns ahead. An amusing collection dance for the rook!

Two rooks on the seventh rank can be a most powerful weapon.

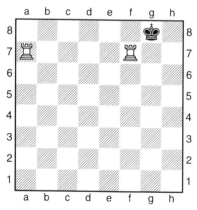

Two ideas are always present:

a) The possibility of threatening mate on the back rank with, for example, 1 ♖fb7.

b) The possibility of forcing a draw by perpetual check; e.g., 1 ♖g7+ ♔f8 2 ♖gf7+ ♔e8 3 ♖fe7+, etc.

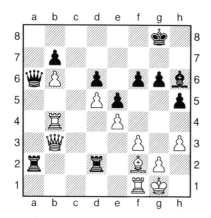

This is the game Gheorghiu vs Diez del Corral at Las Palmas in 1973. Play continued:

1...♕xf1+ 2 ♔xf1 ♖xf2+ *(D)*

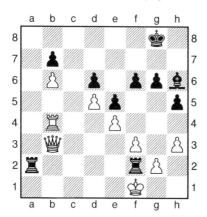

3 ♔g1

3 ♔e1 ♖xg2 4 ♔f1 ♖gc2 leads to the same thing.

3...♖xg2+ 4 ♔h1 ♖gc2

White now resigned since he will have to give up his queen to avoid mate.

Try for Yourself 23

In the upper diagram in the right-hand column of page 82, Antunac has just played 5 ♖xh7+. Instead he could have been greedy!

He could have picked up another pawn with 5 ♖xa7+ before winning the white queen. Why didn't he?

Try for Yourself 24

Antunac probably borrowed his idea from Carlos Torre, who as White pulled off a spectacular victory over former world champion Emanuel Lasker from this position at Moscow in 1925.

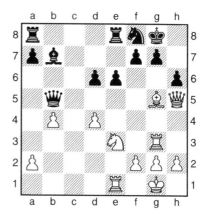

Think about the Antunac vs Hübner game and see if you can find the move that led to a similar rook dance.

(The solutions are on pages 93-4.)

38 Bishop or Knight?

Which is worth more, a bishop or a knight?

We gave them each a bank value of about three points. But can they really be equal when their moves are so different?

The bishop can strike from long range but only on squares of one colour.

The knight can use both light and dark squares but is slow and rather clumsy moving around the board.

They can't be exactly equal.

So which is better?

It all depends upon the position!

Bishops need an open board. To develop their full firepower they need diagonals that are not blocked by pawns.

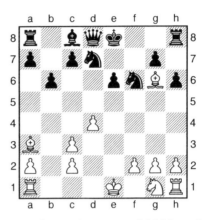

Open diagonals = powerful bishops!

In the next position, from the game Sokolsky vs Saigin at Kiev in 1950, Black's bishops are biting on concrete.

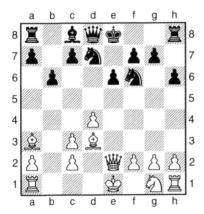

In this position the white bishops are magnificent pieces. The d3-bishop has two fine lines of attack towards a6 and h7. The a3-bishop cuts right into Black's position and by hitting f8 is preventing him from castling.

The game Alekhine vs Vasić from a simultaneous display at Banja Luka in 1931 ended dramatically: **1 ♕xe6+! fxe6 2 ♗g6#** *(D)*.

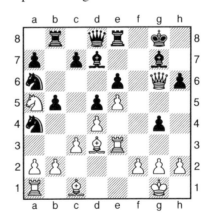

The d7-bishop is blocked by its own pawns on e6 and b5. The g7-bishop is blocked by its own pawn on h6 and the white e5-pawn. In comparison, the white bishops have great freedom and it is no surprise that Sokolsky won at once with **1 ♖f3!**, opening the diagonal of the c1-bishop and threatening 2 ♕h7#.

Black resigned after **1...gxf3 2 ♗xh6** *(D)*.

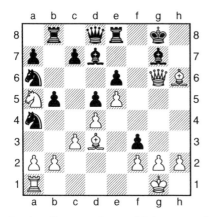

As the diagram shows, bishops can be, like White's, very good. However, they can also be like Black's – very bad!

Bishops can be pieces of extremes. In contrast, knights are more average but the next position shows them at their best.

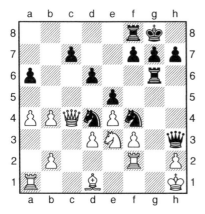

The chains of pawns rather block the position and White's pieces lack good open lines. However, the black knights are powerful pieces. They work well as a pair and can manoeuvre easily in this *closed position*. They have good solid bases from which to operate and it is difficult for White to dislodge them. The game Pegoraro vs Scheipel, Strasbourg 1971 concluded **1...♖g3! 2 ♖c1 ♘xf3 3 ♗b3 ♖g2 4 ♖xg2 ♘xg2 5 ♘f1 ♘e3!** *(D)*, when the black cavalry hits everything in sight: g2, h2, the white queen, c2, the white knight...!

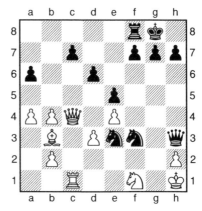

Not surprisingly it was *good knight* as far as White was concerned. Faced with so many threats, he resigned!

You must always consider the nature of the position before exchanging bishops and knights.

Remember also that the bishop is always likely to be a little stronger on an open board. Therefore at the beginning of the game it is usually better not to exchange a bishop for a knight unless you have a good reason for doing so.

39 The Bad Bishop

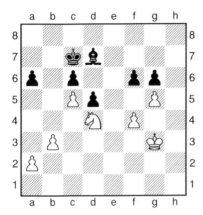

Averbakh has just played 1 g5 in his game with Lilienthal at Moscow in 1949. Can you think why?

Although the bank value of the pieces is equal, the practical value of White's knight is much greater than Black's bishop. This becomes most obvious after **1...f5** *(D)*.

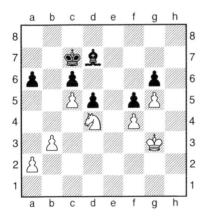

Black's poor bishop is buried alive. All the pawns stand on light squares and four of them are blocked, fixed to the spot. The white knight has a perfect dark-squared base from which it cannot be dislodged. It can also

manoeuvre easily to e5, which might be an even better base.

2 ♘f3 ♗e8 3 ♘e5

Black's c6- and g6-pawns don't just get in the way of their bishop, they make great targets for the white knight and the poor bishop has to defend them.

White now needs to improve the position of his king; d4 will be a good square, and e5 an even better one. From e5 the white king will be threatening to invade on d6 and f6 to mop up Black's miserable pawns. (Notice how all White's target squares, d4, e5, f6 and d6, are *dark squares*.)

3...♔d8 4 ♔f3 ♔e7 5 ♔e3 ♔e6 6 ♔d4 ♔e7 7 ♘d3 ♔e6 *(D)*

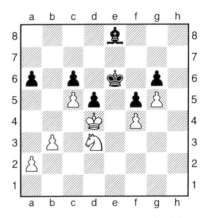

Black is totally tied up. His king must stay on e6 to prevent the white king from invading on e5. His bishop must shuffle around d7, e8 and f7 in order to be able to defend the c6- and g6-pawns.

Now White can break through on the queenside:

8 ♘b4 a5 9 ♘d3 ♗d7 10 a4 ♗e8 11 b4 axb4 12 ♘xb4 *(D)*

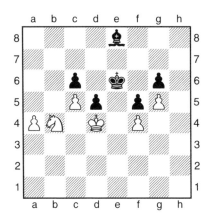

And Black loses because when his king runs across to stop White's a-pawn, he leaves his front door open and the white king marches in through e5.

In the game Lilienthal didn't play 1...f5. He went for the other option: **1...fxg5 2 fxg5 ♗c8 3 ♔f4** *(D)* and here Black resigned.

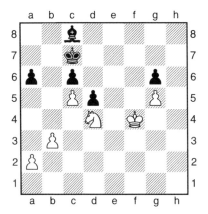

After **3...a5 4 ♔e5 ♗g4 5 ♔f6 ♗h5** the g6-pawn is dreadfully weak. White can now switch the point of attack to the c6-pawn and overload the poor bishop with defensive work: **6 ♔e7 ♗g4 7 a3 ♗d1** (Black has got some play for his bishop but it is too little and too late) **8 ♘e6+ ♔b7 9 ♔d6 ♗xb3 10 ♘d8+ ♔c8 11 ♘xc6 a4 12 ♘e7+** *(D)*.

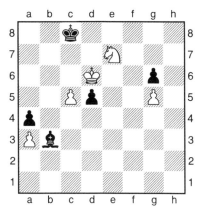

White's c5-pawn will soon queen.

So, have you worked it out? Why did Averbakh play **1 g5**?

To fix the black pawn on g6!

Pawns restrict the power of bishops. With his pawns blockaded on c6, d5 and g6 Lilienthal's bishop was a very *bad bishop* indeed!

Don't allow too many of your pawns to become fixed on the same coloured squares as a bishop ... and if you do, look for a way to exchange the bishop.

Bishops need open diagonals!

40 The Two Bishops

You may hear strong players talking about *having the two bishops*. While analysing and judging a position, one of them might say White has *the advantage of the two bishops*.

What does this mean? What is the advantage of having two bishops?

Well, two bishops working together on an open board control squares of both colours. They are a powerful weapon and are likely to be worth more than a bishop and knight.

Let's see! Sit back and enjoy two games, taking note of how Black's bishops combine to control a whole block of squares.

The first game was played between Chepukaitis and Yakovliev in 1981 in Leningrad. The moves **1 d4 ♘f6 2 ♗g5 ♘e4 3 ♗h4 d5 4 f3 g5 5 fxe4 gxh4 6 exd5 ♕xd5 7 ♘c3 ♕a5 8 ♘f3 h3 9 g3 ♗h6 10 ♕d3 ♘c6 11 e4 ♗g4 12 ♘d2?** *(D)* bring us to the following position:

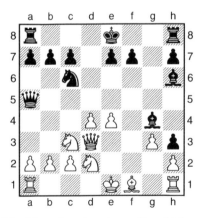

Black has *the advantage of two bishops* for a bishop and a knight on an open board. They scythe across it with deadly effect. Black finished off brilliantly: **12...♘b4 13 ♕b5+ c6!!** *(D)*.

White was expecting 13...♕xb5 14 ♗xb5+ c6 15 ♗a4, when he defends the important square c2 and has made some space for his king.

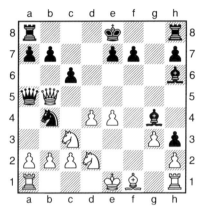

White now resigned as **14 ♕xa5 ♘xc2+ 15 ♔f2 ♗e3#** *(D)* is mate.

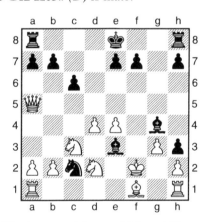

The beauty of the two bishops! They combine to trap the white king in a neat block of squares.

At Breslau in 1862 the game Rosanes vs Anderssen began **1 e4 e5 2 f4 d5 3 exd5 e4 4**

♗b5+ c6 5 dxc6 ♘xc6 6 ♘c3 ♘f6 7 ♕e2
♗c5! 8 ♘xe4 0-0 (D).

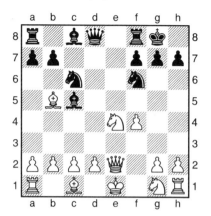

White has two pawns – and a problem!
Black's pieces are very active, in particular
the c6-knight which threatens to leap into
d4. White decides the knight must go.

9 ♗xc6

Giving up the bishop has major reper-
cussions, but 9 ♘xc5? ♖e8 costs White his
queen.

**9...bxc6 10 d3 ♖e8 11 ♗d2 ♘xe4 12
dxe4 ♗f5! 13 e5 ♕b6** (D)

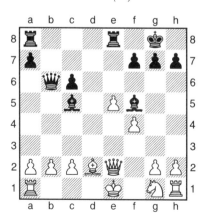

When he played 9 ♗xc6, White handed his
opponent the two bishops. Now just look at
them! Both occupy splendid diagonals and
threaten to win material.

14 0-0-0 ♗d4!

Now the bishops work as a pair! They
smash into the white king's pawn-shield.

15 c3 ♖ab8! 16 b3 ♖ed8

In fact, 16...♕a5! is a clearer win.

17 ♘f3

After 17 cxd4 ♕xd4 White cannot prevent
mate on a1. 17 g4 is necessary, but also grim
for White.

17...♕xb3!!

The queen is sacrificed to strip the king bare
and make way for the rooks and bishops.

18 axb3 ♖xb3 19 ♗e1 ♗e3+ (D)

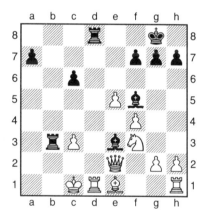

Black's rooks control the files and his bishops the diagonals. The squares around White's
king are all covered. Game over! **White resigned** because 20 ♕xe3 ♖b1# is mate.

On an open board, two bishops are a powerful weapon because they can control both
light and dark squares.

41 Outposts

An *outpost* is a square in your opponent's half of the board that you can control but which can never be attacked by an enemy pawn. *Outposts* can make marvellous bases for pieces!

Can you spot White's *outpost* square in this position and work out how he makes best use of it?

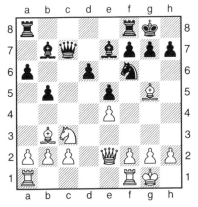

First, d5 is White's *outpost*. A piece on d5 will be defended by White's e4-pawn and no black pawn will be able to attack it.

Second, whilst *outposts* can be used by all pieces, they make particularly good bases for knights. The reason is that the knight is a short-range piece which does not have much influence on the enemy position when it is on the third rank. It's a different story when the knight occupies an advanced square.

In our position the c3-knight would like to seize the d5 *outpost* square but he has competition from the black bishop and knight. So, with **1 ♗xf6 ♗xf6 2 ♗d5** White exchanges the pieces and d5 falls into his hands; e.g., **2...♖ac8 3 ♗xb7 ♕xb7 4 ♘d5** *(D)*.

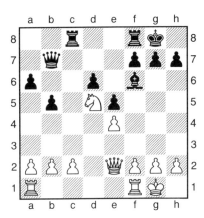

The knight is dominant and it cannot be removed from its splendid *outpost*.

John Emms gave a good demonstration of the power of an *outpost* knight in his game with Keogh in Dublin in 1991:

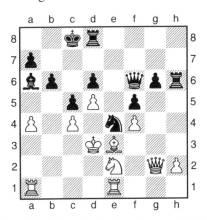

The black knight is dug in beautifully on e4. Emms played **1...♕b2!** and because his knight is attacking d2 and c3 he has the nasty threat of 2...♕b3+ mating.

White has no defence. He played **2 ♖eb1 ♗xc4+ 3 ♔xc4**, when Black's quickest way to force mate is to continue 3...b5+! 4 axb5 ♕c2+.

"Once you get a knight firmly posted on e6, you may go to sleep. Your game will play itself." So said the tactical genius Adolf Anderssen more than a century ago.

John Emms followed step one in his game against Miroslav Houska at London in 1999. His knight is beautifully posted on e6...

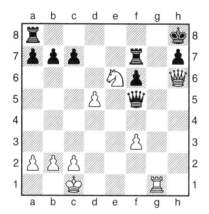

...but he certainly wasn't asleep when he found **1 ♖g7! ♖g8 2 ♘d4!** *(D)*. Don't forget that pieces can move backwards!

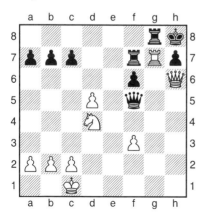

Black has to give up his queen or be mated on h7.

It is a good idea throughout the game to try to imagine the board without any of the pieces, and with just the kings and pawns in place. There are many advantages to this idea.

You will be able to assess what is likely to happen if pieces are exchanged and an endgame arises.

You will see which bishops will have open diagonals and which will turn out to be bad bishops.

And you will also highlight any *outpost* squares and be able to consider how you might use them. Remember this when you tackle this next problem:

Try for Yourself 25

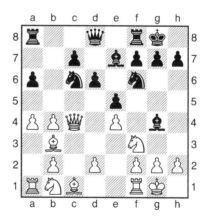

With his next move Black took control of one *outpost* and created another one for himself. What move did he play?

When Black had created his second *outpost*, what did he need to do before occupying it with a knight?

(The answer is on page 94.)

42 Underpromotion

When you get a pawn to the far end of the board you exchange it for a queen.

Right? Wrong!

When you get a pawn to the far end of the board you can choose to *promote* it to *any other piece* of the same colour (except a king!).

Sometimes in the endgame if you take a queen you might leave your opponent stalemated. In this case you might consider promoting to a rook.

Sometimes you might choose a minor piece, as we shall see.

I came across two old gentlemen playing chess on a park bench in Leningrad in 1974. Through a fog of cigarette smoke Black played ...g3 to reach this position:

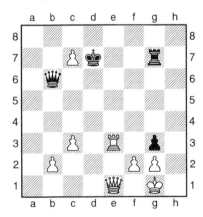

Without a great deal of thought White bashed out **1 ♖e7+ ♖xe7 2 ♕xe7+ ♔xe7**. Oops, I thought, he's blundered. White then surveyed his audience – that was me, a dog and a couple of hooded crows – he smiled, said something in my direction which meant as much to the dog and its feathered friends as it did to me, and pushed **3 c8** *(D)*.

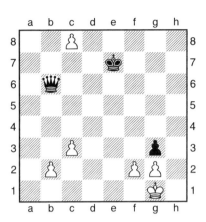

With the pawn still on c8, Black picked up his king, twirled it in his fingers for a few moments, shrugged his shoulders and began resetting the pieces for another game. Black had resigned!

I gave a puzzled look and wandered off shaking my head. A few yards down the path the light dawned.

As I turned smiling, White looked up, picked up a knight and gave me a polite bow of his head.

My problem was that I had only considered **3 c8♕**, when **3...♕xf2+ 4 ♔h1 ♕f1#** is mate.

I had missed **3 c8♘+!**. Promoting to a knight is *check*! And on c8 the knight forks Black's king and queen.

Normally you will want to take a queen when you *promote* a pawn. But remember you are not forced to. Remember you have a choice. Remember stalemate. Remember a knight promotion might be check, and that could make a decisive difference.

Remember underpromotion!

Try for Yourself Solutions

20)

1 d5? is a dreadful move. It completely blocks the line of the g2-bishop and leaves White's queen and rook with nothing to do on the d-file.

White has a lead in development and his pieces are screaming out for lines and space, so 1 dxe5, opening the d-file, is a must! If then 1...dxe5?, 2 ♕d8+ wins a rook.

For Black, the last thing he wants is to open lines since it is White's pieces which are already in position to use them. Black must avoid pawn exchanges. He should play 1...e4 blunting the g2-bishop and keeping lines closed.

21)

Tal probably gave no thought to his back rank as his king has an escape square on h7. However, this square will be attacked by the d3-bishop when the e4-rook moves. Olafsson played 1 ♕xc8+ and Tal had to resign since 1...♗xc8 2 ♖e8# is mate.

22)

Teschner realized that he had everything under control on the c- and e-files. He knew his queen would be safe after 1 ♖xd5 because 1...♖xc2? is answered by 2 ♖xe8+ and mate on the back rank. He also knew he had a back-rank mate after 1...♖xe2? 2 ♕xc8#.

Happy with his calculations, Teschner continued 1 ♖xd5?. Obligingly, Portisch played 1...♕a6 and after 2 ♘g3 the game was later drawn.

What both players missed was the astonishing 1...♕f2!! *(D)*, placing the queen

en prise but threatening mate on f1 and the rook on e2.

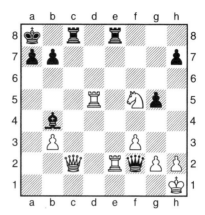

White can resign since both 2 ♖xf2 ♖e1+ and 2 ♘g3 ♕e1+ have the same result: mate on the back rank!

23)

After 5 ♖xa7+ ♔e8 6 ♖e7+ ♔f8 7 ♖xh7+ Black does not continue the same dance with 7...♔e8. Instead he uses the fact that the a7-pawn has disappeared to play 7...♖xa3! 8 ♖xh5 ♖xa2, when suddenly Black comes out a piece up.

24)

Torre sacrificed his queen with 1 ♗f6! ♕xh5. As his own queen was *en prise* on b5, Black's only alternative is 1...g5 when he is mated on g7 after 2 ♕xh6. Now Torre played 2 ♖xg7+ ♔h8 and then not 3 ♖g5+, regaining the queen immediately, but the collection dance of 3 ♖xf7+ ♔g8 4 ♖g7+ ♔h8 5 ♖xb7+ ♔g8 6 ♖g7+ ♔h8. Having picked up two pawns and a bishop, Torre went back for the queen with 7 ♖g5+ ♔h7 8 ♖xh5 *(D)*. Well done if you worked that out.

But wait a minute! Have you looked further?

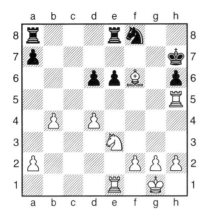

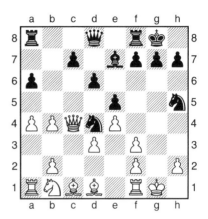

As we have seen before, it is very easy to stop analysing at a point like this without looking to see what happens next. The combination appears to be over. White has won his material, and that is surely the end of the matter!

No, you cannot stop before you have looked to see if there is a sting in the tail. And there is!

Black can spoil the fun with **8...♗g6** forking rook and bishop. However, after **9 ♖h3 ♔xf6 10 ♖xh6+ ♔g5 11 ♖h3** there is no further sting and Lasker resigned, as Black is simply three pawns down.

25)

Black has an *outpost* square on d4 and a knight on c6 ready to pounce. First he needs to deal with the defender, White's f3-knight. Black played **1...♗xf3 2 gxf3** (White would drop a pawn with 2 ♕xc6 ♗xe4) **2...♘d4**. Black has not only secured d4, but has also created a second *outpost* square on f4. Play continued **3 ♗d1 ♘h5 4 d3** *(D)*.

Black has moved his knight to h5 but he needs to get rid of White's c1-bishop before the knight can occupy f4.

4...♗g5! 5 ♔h1 ♗f4. The bishop uses the *outpost*! Black is threatening 6...♕h4 and mate on h2 so White is forced to exchange: **6 ♗xf4 ♘xf4** *(D)*.

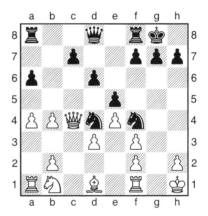

Mighty knights on mighty *outposts*!

(If you look back to the game Pegoraro vs Scheipel in '**38**' you will see how the knights finished White off.)

6 The Pawns

"Pawns," said André-François Danican Philidor, the greatest player of the 18th century, "are the soul of chess."

It is the pawns that give the game its shape. It is the pawns that can help you to control space. It is the pawns that can open or close lines to give power to the pieces.

Throughout the game you should be constantly thinking about the position of your pawns and how they affect your pieces. You should remember the one peculiarity of the pawn: unlike the pieces, it cannot move backwards. A pawn move is a move for ever.

43 Pawn-Structure

If you look at the lovely open files and diagonals White has for his three pieces in the diagram below you won't be surprised that he can win immediately:

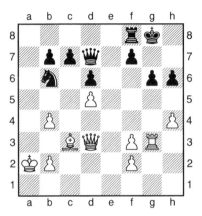

The sacrifice **1 ♖xg6+!** rips apart Black's defences and forces mate in a few moves: **1...fxg6** (or 1...♔h7 2 ♖g7+ ♔h8 3 ♕h7#) **2 ♕xg6+ ♕g7 3 ♕xg7#** *(D)*.

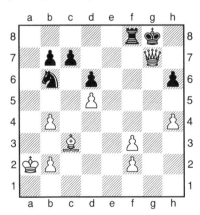

The open lines enabled White's attack to hammer home!

However, open lines are only useful if we have pieces that can make use of them.

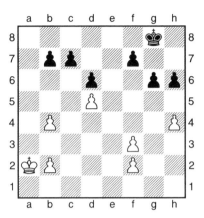

In this diagram, the *pawn-structure* is the same as before so White still has his open files and diagonals but now he doesn't have any pieces to make use of them!

The game might continue **1 ♔b3 ♔g7 2 ♔c3 ♔f6 3 ♔d4 ♔f5** *(D)*.

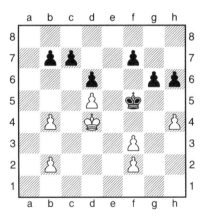

White has a problem!

Black has the simple plan of 4...♔f4, 5...♔xf3, 6...♔xf2, 7...♔g3 and 8...f5, after which his f-pawn promotes. He can even play ...♔xh4 if he is feeling greedy!

How can White prevent Black's plan?

Only by **4 ♔e3**, after which Black plays 4...♔e5 and 5...♔xd5 and wins easily.

Let's put the minor pieces back on:

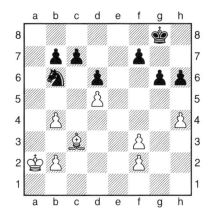

White still has a problem!

His d5-pawn is *en prise* and he has no way of defending it! The pawn is doomed. Black is winning easily again.

OK! Let's get rid of the minor pieces and the two kings:

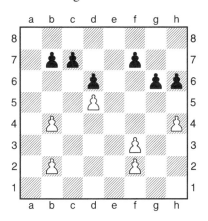

This represents the *pawn-structure* of the position.

Pawn-structure is important because it is the position of the pawns which gives the pieces their power.

At some stage White played d5, opening the diagonal for his bishop on c3.

At some stage White played g2xf3, opening the g-file for his rook.

With pieces on the board, White used the open diagonal and the open file for his mating attack.

Pawn-structure is important because pawns are valuable. Lose your pawns and you will lose the endgame! With the pieces off the board, White would lose the endgame because he cannot defend his pawns. He would also lose with bishop against knight because he can't defend the d5-pawn.

Every time you push a pawn forward one square, you open and block diagonals for your queen and bishops. Every time you make a pawn capture, you open and block files for your queen and rooks.

Pawns can't move backwards, so if you later regret a pawn move there is nothing you can do about it.

In your games you must keep an eye on your *pawn-structure* all the time. Make sure your pawns are helping your pieces but don't let them become scattered targets of attack. Look after your pawns.

44 Weak Pawns

In the pawn-structure position from '**43**' Black has two nice, neat and tidy groups, or *islands*, of pawns:

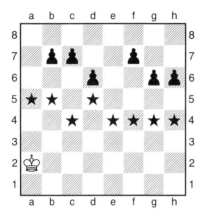

The white king cannot advance further than the barrier of squares marked with a star so he cannot get *into* Black's position to attack and capture any of the pawns.

However, for the black king there is no barrier!

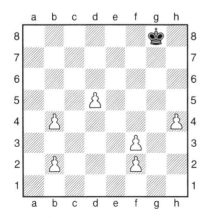

The white pawns are scattered into four *pawn-islands* and the black king is free to wander wherever he likes. He can sail off to the first *island* and gobble up the h4-pawn before moving to the second *island* and devouring the f2- and f3-pawns. The b2- and b4- *island* might come next and finally he can sunbathe in splendour on d5, king of the board!

White's pawns are all weak because they are *isolated*. An *isolated pawn* is one that does not have a pawn of the same colour on the files either side of it. The d5-pawn is *isolated* because there is no white pawn on either the c- or the e-file. The b2- and b4-pawns are *doubled isolated pawns*. They are *doubled* because there are two of them on the same file and *isolated* because there are no white pawns on the a- or c-files.

I made up the pawn-structure in '**43**' to show both the power of the open lines and the weakness of the pawns. The next position shows the problem of an *isolated pawn* in a real game.

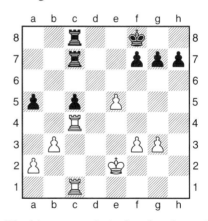

Black's c-pawn is *isolated* and attacked. Because it is *isolated* it cannot be defended by another pawn; it has to be defended by pieces. In the diagram, two white rooks are attacking the c5-pawn so two black rooks are having to defend.

It might seem a fair balance, but it isn't! Whilst Black's rooks are tied to defending the pawn, White's rooks are free to move wherever they wish, whenever they wish. White's rooks do not *have* to attack the pawn but Black's rooks *must* defend. White can play ♖h4, ♖a4 or ♖h1 to attack another black pawn or he can use the rooks for other plans.

Black cannot do anything with his rooks. If he plays 1...♖e7 to attack the e5-pawn, White simply plays 2 ♖xc5. He captures the pawn, he defends his own e5-pawn and he attacks Black's other weak *isolated pawn* on a5.

In the next position Black doesn't have an *isolated pawn* but he does have something that can be just as big a problem – a *backward pawn*.

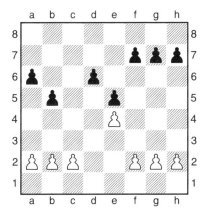

The black pawn on d6 is a *backward pawn*. It can never be defended by another

pawn because there is no black pawn on the c-file and because it is behind (or *backward* of) the e5-pawn.

Of course if the d6-pawn could safely move to d5 there would be no problem but as we saw in the position in '**41**', White will if at all possible make jolly sure it remains *backward*.

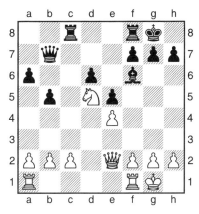

The d5-square is attacked by the e4-pawn and occupied by the white knight. Black has no hope of playing ...d5. One good plan now for White would be to put his rooks on d3 and d1. He would be piling up pressure on the d6-pawn and be threatening to move his knight. Black would have to begin defending the d6-pawn. Then with the black pieces tied down to defence, White might switch to an attack on the black king with ♖g3 and ♕g4.

Of course you will have more to worry about in a game than just the position of your pawns, but remember that if you lose a pawn you may well lose the endgame – and weak pawns are easily lost!

45 Holes

Holes are weak squares – potential outposts for pieces to occupy. They are squares in the pawn-structure that can never be defended by a pawn.

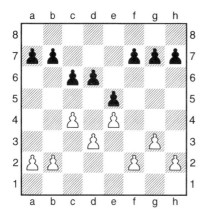

In this position White has three *holes*, the squares d4, f3 and h3.

The problem with *holes* is that they invite enemy pieces to invade them, as in this diagram:

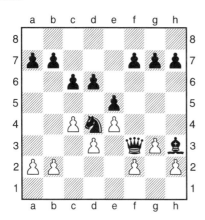

If Black managed to achieve this piece formation, then a white king on g1 would be in rather a lot of trouble!

Holes in the king's pawn-shield can be really disastrous and you should always try to avoid weakening your shield.

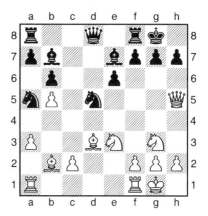

In this position, from the game Spielmann vs Honlinger played at Vienna in 1929, White has just played ♕h5, threatening mate on h7.

Honlinger should have blocked the white bishop's diagonal with 17...f5. Instead he weakened his pawn-shield with **17...g6?** and was stunned by **18 ♘g4!!** *(D)*.

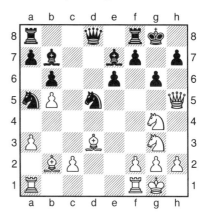

The holes on f6 and h6 are gaping. If now 18...gxh5, 19 ♘h6# is mate. Honlinger noticed that if he tried 18...♘f6 19 ♕e5 ♚g7, he would be hammered on f6 by 20 ♘h5+!! *(D)*.

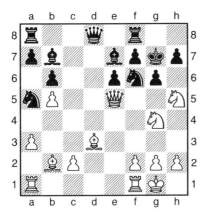

To avoid immediate disaster, Honlinger had to try **18...♗f6** but this also has a disadvantage. He really wants to keep the bishop since it works on dark squares and is the best piece with which to defend his miserable *holes*. Spielmann did not think twice about chopping the bishop off: **19 ♘xf6+ ♘xf6 20 ♕h6** *(D)*.

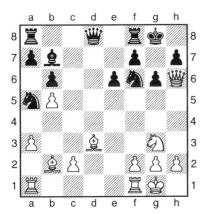

With *holes* on f6 and h6 and no dark-squared bishop, Black has real problems!

A few moves later, the following position was reached:

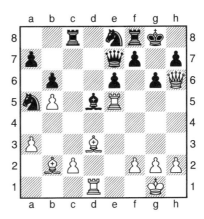

Black is desperately trying to defend his dark squares f6 and g7. If he had time now to play ...f6 he might survive.

However, he doesn't!

It was Spielmann's move and he finished off spectacularly with **26 ♕xh7+!! ♚xh7 27 ♖h5+ ♚g8 28 ♖h8#**, making full use of the power of the two bishops.

You should generally try to avoid making *holes* in your pawn-structure. You should be particularly careful not to weaken the pawn-shield in front of your king.

Similarly, you should be on the lookout for *holes* in your opponent's position and for ways of occupying them. You should try to tempt your opponent to advance a pawn in front of his king.

You should remember that the bishop is generally the best piece to defend weak squares in a pawn-shield. Exchange your opponent's defensive bishop if you are attacking, and hang on to your own bishop if it is you that has the *holes*.

46 Doubled Pawns

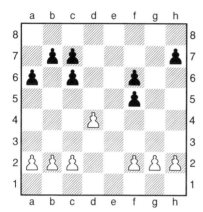

In this pawn-structure diagram, Black has *doubled pawns* on c6 and c7.

Do you think that is a problem?

Are the pawns weak?

No, not really.

Black's queenside pawn-island forms a nice solid block. The c7-pawn is a bit of a problem because it is stuck on the c7-square blocked by the c6-pawn. If it is attacked, it can't escape by advancing; it will have to be defended by a piece. However, whilst the c7-pawn may be a bit of a problem, Black has compensation in the form of the d-file, which he can use for his rook or queen.

Remember: if you have *doubled pawns* then you must also have an open file!

Black's f5- and f6-pawns are also *doubled*.

Do you think that is a problem?

Are the pawns weak?

Yes, definitely!

The problem is that the pawns are both *doubled* and *isolated*. Yes, Black does have the g-file as a line of attack for a rook but the

pawns themselves cause the same problems as all *isolated pawns* – only now there are two of them!

They will be targets for attack and they will become more and more of a headache as the endgame approaches.

The main problem with *doubled pawns* usually comes in the endgame.

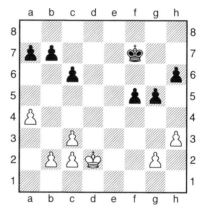

In this position White's *doubled pawns* on the c-file are not weak. OK, the c2-pawn is blocked like Black's c7-pawn in the last position but with only kings on the board it isn't really a target for attack.

White's problem is that he cannot advance his four pawns on the queenside against Black's three and make a passed pawn.

Black, on the other hand, is able to use his *pawn-majority* of three against two to make a passed pawn on the kingside.

From the diagram, play might continue:

1...♔e6 2 ♔e3 ♔e5 3 b4 f4+ 4 ♔f3 ♔f5 5 c4 h5 6 b5 g4+ 7 hxg4+ hxg4+ 8 ♔f2 ♔e4 *(D)*

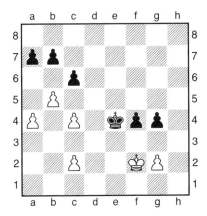

We can see White's problems clearly!

He has been advancing his pawns on the queenside but unless Black makes the mistake of playing ...cxb5, White has no hope of making a passed pawn. If White tries 9 a5 intending 10 a6!, Black just blocks him with 9...a6 and there is no way through. White's extra c2-pawn is useless so he is effectively playing with three pawns against three on that side of the board.

On the other side Black has advanced his three pawns against White's two and although the white king has been trying desperately to slow them down, Black is ready to play 8...f3 and create his own passed pawn.

Black's position is now actually so strong that he can afford to abandon his f4- and g4-pawns and use his king to gobble up all of White's pawns on the queenside.

Doubled pawns will cost White the game. His c2-pawn is of no help so he is really playing just a pawn down.

In the position below we have moved the white pawn from c3 to g3 – and what a difference it makes!

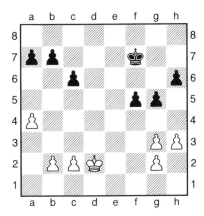

White still has *doubled pawns* but now they don't matter at all because Black no longer has a *pawn-majority* on the kingside and therefore he cannot hope to create a *passed pawn*.

The game might continue as before: **1...♔e6 2 ♔e3 ♔e5** but now 3...f4+ is no longer a dangerous threat because of 4 gxf4+ gxf4+ 5 ♔f3, when there is no passed pawn for Black.

You shouldn't worry too much about getting your pawns *doubled* early in the game. *Doubled pawns* are not as weak as *isolated pawns* and you will get an open file as compensation.

You must still think about the endgame though! Try to avoid getting your pawns *doubled* if it is going to leave your opponent with a *pawn-majority* on the other side of the board which he can use to make a passed pawn.

47 The Isolated Queen's Pawn

The pawn-structure position in the next diagram, in which White has an isolated d-pawn, can arise from many openings.

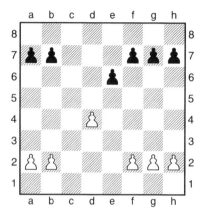

The player with the isolated queen's pawn will often have more space and good attacking chances. He will also be in danger of slipping into a bad ending or of simply losing the pawn.

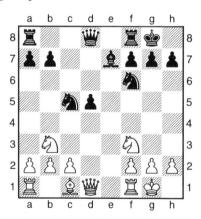

In this example Black's d5-pawn looks safe, defended by both queen and knight. However, Krogius, as White against Boleslavsky at Riga in 1958, played a series of simple, easy-to-understand moves and the d5-pawn just fell like a leaf in autumn.

1 ♘xc5

This draws the black bishop away from e7.

1...♗xc5 2 ♗g5

This pins Black's defending knight. White threatens 3 ♗xf6, when Black must reply with 3...gxf6 since 3...♕xf6 allows 4 ♕xd5. Then Black's bishop would be *en prise* so he would not have time to play 4...♕xb2.

2...♖c8

This defends the bishop so that 3 ♗xf6 ♕xf6 4 ♕xd5 can be answered by 4...♕xb2.

3 c3

This blocks the diagonal from f6 to b2 and threatens 4 ♗xf6 and 5 ♕xd5 all over again.

3...♖c6

This prepares to recapture on f6 with the rook.

4 ♕d3

This prepares to put more pressure on the d5-pawn with 5 ♖ad1.

4...h6 5 ♗xf6 ♖xf6 6 ♖ad1 *(D)*

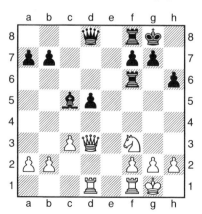

The d5-pawn now drops since 6...♖d6 7 b4 ♗b6 8 c4! is horrible: the d5-pawn is pinned and White threatens 9 c5. Boleslavsky tried **6...♕b6** but lost the pawn and eventually the game after **7 b4 ♗d6 8 ♕xd5**.

In the next position, Viktor Korchnoi's attack with the white pieces had fizzled out and Anatoly Karpov took another step towards retaining his world championship title in Merano in 1981 (this was the ninth match-game) by laying siege to an *isolated queen's pawn.*

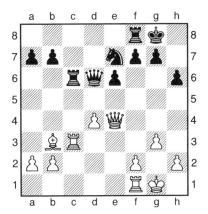

Karpov already has the important d5-square firmly under control. Now he begins the process of attacking the d4-pawn.

1...♖d8 2 ♖d1

The pawn cannot advance so it must be defended.

2...♖b6 3 ♕e1 ♕d7 4 ♖cd3 ♖d6 5 ♕e4 ♕c6

The more pieces that are exchanged, the weaker the d4-pawn will become.

6 ♕f4 ♘d5

The strongpoint is occupied!

7 ♕d2 ♕b6

This threatens 8...♘b4, winning the d4-pawn after the rook moves from d3.

8 ♗xd5 ♖xd5

The strongpoint is still occupied.

9 ♖b3 ♕c6 10 ♕c3 ♕d7 *(D)*

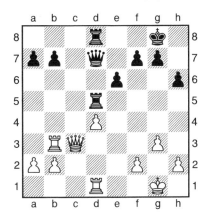

Now Karpov has the simple threat of 11...e5 as the wretched d4-pawn is pinned to his rook.

11 f4

This is the only way White can save his d4-pawn but it opens up lines to his king. Meanwhile the d4-pawn remains a target.

11...b6 12 ♖b4 b5

Threatening 13...a5 14 ♖b3 b4 followed by 15...♖xd4.

13 a4 bxa4 14 ♕a3 a5 15 ♖xa4 ♕b5 16 ♖d2 e5! 17 fxe5 ♖xe5 *(D)*

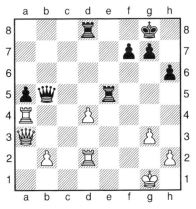

This threatens 18...♖e1+ 19 ♔g2 ♕f1#.

18 ♕a1

The d4-pawn is still a problem. After 18 dxe5 ♖xd2 Black threatens both 19...♕e2 and 19...♕b6+.

18...♕e8! 19 dxe5 ♖xd2 20 ♖xa5 *(D)*

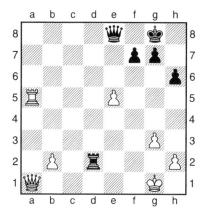

Korchnoi has got rid of his *isolated queen's pawn* and he's even won a pawn into the bargain. Life would be good – if he didn't have a king to worry about!

20...♕c6 21 ♖a8+ ♔h7 22 ♕b1+ g6 23 ♕f1 ♕c5+ 24 ♔h1 ♕d5+

Korchnoi resigned owing to 25 ♔g1 ♖d1 winning the queen.

When your opponent has an *isolated queen's pawn* your own general plan of action will be:

a) To control and occupy the strongpoint square in front of the *isolated pawn*, blockading the pawn so that it cannot advance.

b) To build up pressure on the *isolated pawn* and tie your opponent's pieces down to defending it.

c) To look for ways of switching to an attack elsewhere when your opponent's pieces are tied to the pawn.

d) To exchange pieces because the pawn will become weaker and a bigger problem for your opponent as the endgame draws closer.

But it is not all doom and gloom if you have an *isolated queen's pawn*. The pawn may be a weakness but it can also be a strength! It gives you more space and the chance to attack.

You can also try exchanging the problem pawn. Korchnoi ignored this idea earlier in his game when he reached this position:

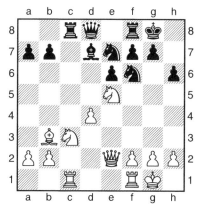

The one thing Korchnoi doesn't want to do is to exchange pieces, yet he played **16 ♘e4 ♘xe4 17 ♕xe4 ♗c6 18 ♘xc6 ♖xc6** *(D)*, which ended his attacking chances.

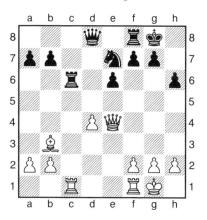

The one thing Korchnoi does want to do now is to exchange his *isolated pawn*. He could have tried 19 ♖xc6, when after 19...♘xc6? (however, 19...bxc6! is still good for Black), 20 d5 gets rid of his problem. Instead he played **19 ♖c3**.

The pawn break d5 is often the key to White's attacking chances as well. Future world champion Boris Spassky gave a good demonstration when he was only twelve against Avtonomov in Leningrad in 1949.

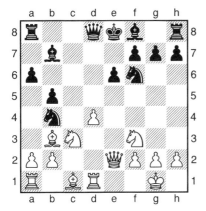

It looks as though Black has the d5-square firmly under his control, yet Spassky still played...

1 d5!

Black must capture because he can't allow 2 dxe6, discovering an attack on his queen.

1...♘bxd5 2 ♗g5

Black is caught in a net of pins: neither knight can move and his e6-pawn is not defending d5. Spassky threatens simply 3 ♘xd5 winning a piece.

2...♗e7 3 ♗xf6! gxf6

Forced as 3...♗xf6 allows 4 ♘xd5.

4 ♘xd5 ♗xd5 5 ♗xd5 exd5 6 ♘d4! *(D)*

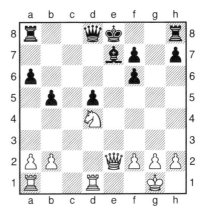

Now, rather amusingly, it is Avtonomov who has the *isolated queen's pawn* and Spassky who has the strongpoint square d4 as a superb base for his knight. Spassky also has the f5-square in front of the doubled isolated f-pawns and for this reason Black cannot castle. After 6...0-0 7 ♘f5 White threatens both 8 ♘xe7+ and 8 ♕g4+ mating. The game ended quickly: **6...♔f8 7 ♘f5 h5 8 ♖xd5! ♕xd5 9 ♕xe7+ ♔g8 10 ♕xf6** and Black resigned.

Look back to the starting position in Spassky's game and see the chances White has for an attack. He has a queen and a rook on good central files. He has a bishop striking across d5 at e6. He has another bishop ready to come to g5 to annoy the f6-knight. He has a knight ready to leap into e5. He has another knight ready to support the d5 pawn-break. And he has the d4-pawn standing proudly in the middle of the board controlling e5 and c5 and bursting to march forward to d5. Great attacking possibilities!

48 Hanging Pawns

In the diagram below, the white pawns on c4 and d4 are called *hanging pawns*. *Hanging pawns* are a pair standing side by side, alone, without the support of pawns on the files either side of them.

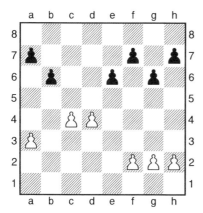

Are the *hanging pawns* in the diagram above strong or weak? What do you think? And how about Black's c- and d-pawns in the position below? Are they strong or will they become a problem?

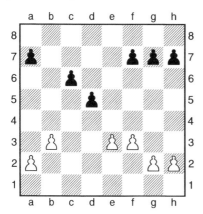

We can see the strength of the *hanging pawns* in the top diagram. Side by side they

are like a spearhead. They attack the squares b5, c5, d5 and e5, preventing Black from putting a piece on any of them. They create space and provide cover for White's pieces. They burst with energy, eager to leap forward. Think about all this as we put some pieces on the board.

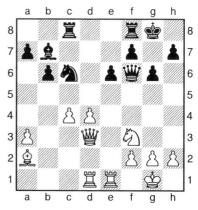

This is Suba vs Velikov from the Lucerne Olympiad, 1982. You can see the *hanging pawns* spearheading White's position, his pieces nicely placed behind them waiting for the breakthrough.

What move do you think White should play? 1 c5 or 1 d5?

After 1 c5 bxc5 2 dxc5 White has opened the d-file for his queen and rook and the diagonal from a2 for his bishop. However, Black can challenge the queen with 2...♖fd8 and the bishop is hitting a brick wall on e6. Worse, the exchange has left White with a single isolated pawn, which is nicely blockaded by Black's knight.

The correct idea is to play **1 d5! exd5 2 cxd5 ♘a5 3 ♘e5 ♖cd8 4 ♘g4 ♕g7 5 d6** *(D)*.

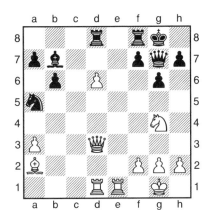

Black has problems! He has to worry about the knight invading his holes on f6 and h6, the rook invading on e7, the possibility of f7 collapsing ... and of course there's the little matter of that rampant d-pawn to frighten him! At least it was all over quickly: **5...♗a8 6 d7 ♘b7 7 ♕e3 h5 8 ♘h6+ ♔h7 9 ♘xf7 ♖xf7 10 ♗xf7 ♕xf7 11 ♕g5** and Black resigned.

Now let's add some pieces to our second pawn-structure position:

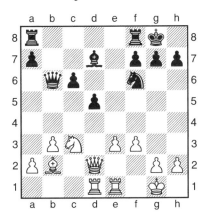

Here the pawns are not *hanging* side by side; one lags behind the other. They do not proudly control the four squares in front of them. The squares that are in front of them, c5 and d4, are no more than holes inviting White's pieces to occupy them. The game Walker vs Blackwell, Oxford 1968 continued **1 ♘a4 ♕d8 2 ♘c5 ♗c8 3 ♕d4** (D).

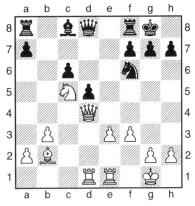

Black has no way of dislodging the white queen and knight and no obvious plan. He is simply being sat upon! He can only wait passively and see how White decides to play to win!

If you have hanging pawns, you should use them as a spearhead of your attack and be on the lookout for the explosive moment to advance one of them and gain more space and attacking power for your pieces.

If your opponent has *hanging pawns*, you should try to attack them head-on so that one of them has to advance at a moment when there is no danger and you can blockade the pair of them.

49 Capturing Towards the Centre

In the diagram below White has just played 1 exf5. How would you recapture? You have four options, but which is best? Do you take with the rook, the bishop, the knight or the pawn?

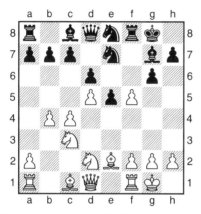

Capturing with 1...Rxf5 does not seem a very bright idea as the rook will soon be a target for the e2-bishop.

Capturing with 1...Bxf5 does look sensible as it develops a piece, and 1...Nxf5 also looks good as the knight may be able to jump into d4 and this move also unclutters Black's position by getting the knight off e7 and out of the way of the black queen.

However, as horrified World Champion-to-be Mikhail Botvinnik commented when the British master Alexander captured with a piece in such a position, "Every Russian schoolboy knows you capture with the pawn!"

So, you should play **1...gxf5!** *(D)*. But why?

Surely on f5 the pawn blocks the f8-rook and the c8-bishop and it deprives the e7-knight of the f5-square.

Surely capturing with the g6-pawn opens up the g-file, at the end of which stands the inviting target of the black king.

Surely capturing with the g6-pawn leaves the h7-pawn isolated and weak.

Yes, all these things are true!

But do they matter? Is there something else more important in the position?

There is!

Remember: *pawns control squares!*

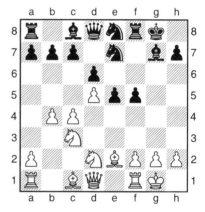

Black's pawn-structure is very good here. Capturing with 1...gxf5 has brought the black g-pawn *towards the centre*.

Side by side, the two black pawns control the four squares in front of them, preventing White from putting a piece on the central squares d4, e4 and f4, and also on g4. A later ...e4 might activate the g7-bishop.

Look again at the pawn-structure after 1 exf5. If Black recaptures with a piece, a white knight will jump into e4 and sit there for a very long time! The e5-pawn will be blockaded. The g7-bishop will be blocked. White will steadily prepare to play c5 and target the squares d6 and c7.

After 1...gxf5 Black can tuck his king away safely in the corner with ...♔h8 and then use the g-file for his own advantage with ...♖g8 bearing down on g2 and the white king. Black can play ...♘g6, freeing his queen and preparing the knight for action on f4 or h4. Black's position has all the ingredients for an attack against the white king and all the time those monster pawns sit side by side controlling squares, controlling space and bursting with energy, straining to leap forward.

A decision you will frequently have to make at the board is how to recapture in positions like the one below.

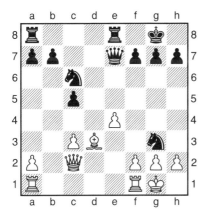

You will often be tempted to retake with the f-pawn as this opens the f-file and gives your rook immediate pressure against f7. Sometimes the open file is really important, but in general the advice is:

Don't!

1 fxg3 splits your pawns into two islands, leaves the e3-square undefended, the e4-pawn isolated and gives Black the beautiful e5-square for his knight!

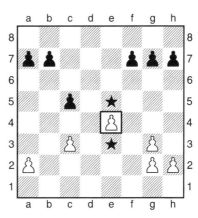

Unless you can see an immediate clear advantage from 1 fxg3, *capturing towards the centre* with **1 hxg3** will almost always be better.

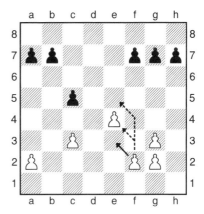

Your kingside pawns are in one island where they will be able to support one another. Your f2-pawn controls e3 and if necessary it can advance to defend the e-pawn or attack the e5-square.

Remember: pawns control squares, and central squares in particular are important. *Capture towards the centre!*

50 Passed Pawns

A *passed pawn* is one that has no enemy pawns obstructing its path to the eighth rank.

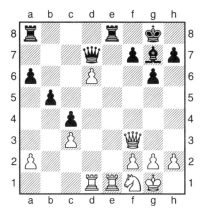

This position is taken from the game Csom vs Ribli at the Hungarian Championship (played in Budapest) in 1969. The white d6-pawn is a *passed pawn* because no black pawn would be able to capture it on its short journey to d8.

The general rule with *passed pawns* is that you should advance them as far and as fast as you can – always provided you are able to defend them. You can't just charge a *passed pawn* up the board and invite your opponent to eat it for breakfast!

Here the d6-pawn is perfectly safe and it acts like a knife at Black's throat.

Your task in this sort of position is to destroy, deflect or block the defenders that obstruct the path of the pawn.

In the game Csom played **1 ≡e7!** threatening both the black queen and 2 ♕xf7+ and mate.

Ribli played **1...♕f5**, whereupon Csom advanced his monster pawn by **2 d7** *(D)* and Ribli resigned.

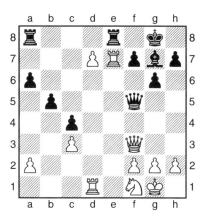

If 2...≡ed8, then 3 ♕xa8! ≡xa8 4 ≡e8+ ≡xe8 5 dxe8♕+ and the little monster has been transformed into a beautiful new queen!

Black's only way of avoiding this would have been **1...≡xe7 2 dxe7**, when he runs into a similar problem: **2...♕e8 3 ♕xa8! ♕xa8 4 ≡d8+** *(D)*, etc.

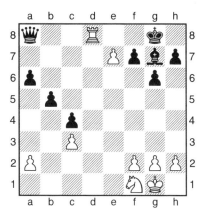

White has destroyed the black rooks and deflected the queen.

The white queen and rooks have done all the damage but the passed d-pawn was the root cause of Black's problems.

In the position below Black creates a *passed pawn* and then blocks the line of the white rook trying to rush back to defend. The game is Rokhlin vs Lohmaya from a match in 1957 between Rostov-on-Don and Tbilisi.

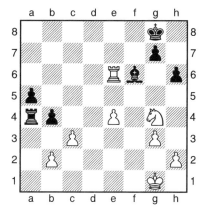

1...♗xc3! 2 bxc3 b3 3 ♖b6 ♖b4!! *(D)*

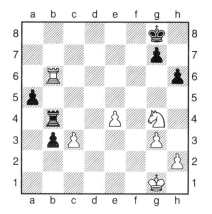

The black rook sacrifices itself in order to block the line between the white rook and the *passed* b3-pawn. After **4 cxb4 a4!** *(D)* not one of White's three pieces can catch the b3-pawn.

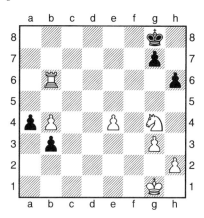

The white king and knight are both too far away to stop the galloping b-pawn promoting.

The white rook is equally useless since **5 ♖d6 b2 6 ♖d1 a3 7 ♖b1 a2** doesn't help White at all.

White can't even bail out into an ending with rook and knight against queen since the black a-pawn is now *passed* and dangerous: **5 ♖a6 b2** and if **6 ♖xa4**, then **6...b1♕+ 7 ♔f2 ♕c2+** forks king and rook.

Pawns may only be worth one point in our banking system but they have the potential to be promoted to a queen (nine points).

Passed pawns are valuable.

Protect them and push them.

Tie your opponent's pieces to blocking their path and then look for tactical ways of dealing with the defenders.

51 The Pawn-Chain

An interlocking line of pawns is known as a *pawn-chain*.

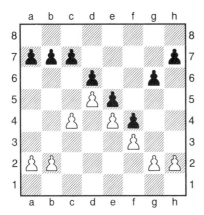

White's *pawn-chain* in this diagram runs from g2 to d5. Black's runs from c7 to f4. *Pawn-chains* tend to be a barrier across the board splitting it into two.

Usually you will attack on the side of the pawn-chain where you have more space and you will expect to defend where your opponent has more room for his pieces to manoeuvre. So in our position White will be likely to advance on the queenside and Black on the kingside.

The general principle is that you should normally try to attack the base of a *pawn-chain*. White's plan here will be to play c5 and exchange pawns on d6. He will then use the open c-file for his queen and rooks, try to invade on c7 and attack d6. Black will play ...g5 and ...g4 and put his major pieces on the g-file. If he exchanges g-pawns, he may be able to use the h3-square for his bishop.

Let's add some pieces and look at a position from a King's Indian Defence.

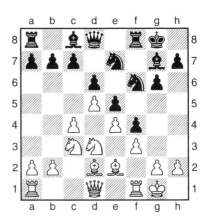

Several games have continued **1 c5 g5 2 ♖c1 ♘g6 3 cxd6 cxd6 4 ♘b5 ♖f7 5 ♕c2** *(D)* and whilst Black is massing for an attack on the white king, White is looking to break through on the queenside.

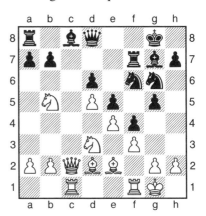

Don't be frightened to advance pawns even in front of your own king. The *pawn-chain* will usually be an effective safety barrier. Remember that you should normally attack the base of your opponent's *chain*.

Now it is about time you did some work!

Try for Yourself 26

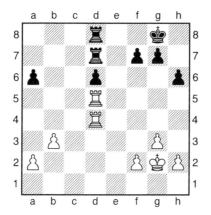

Black's d6-pawn is isolated and weak. But it is safely defended!

Can White win?

Try for Yourself 27

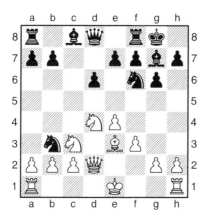

Black has just played ...♘xb3 in this position from the Dragon Variation of the Sicilian Defence.

White has three possible ways to recapture the knight.

Which is best?

Try for Yourself 28

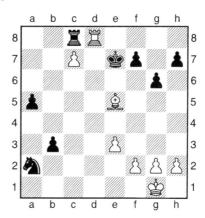

It is Black to play. Both players have passed pawns but only one of them can safely promote. Who, and how? Who is winning?

Try for Yourself 29

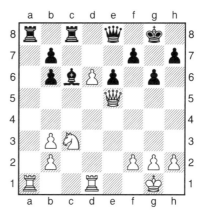

First, you have to study and assess the pawn-structure in this position.

Second, you have to find White's path to victory.

(The solutions are on page 116.)

Try for Yourself Solutions

26)

Always remember that whilst your opponent's pieces may be tied to defending a weak pawn, yours do not necessarily have to attack it.

White wins by switching his point of attack to another weakness, the a6-pawn. And he is spoilt for choice as he has two methods of exploiting this weakness:

a) **1 ♖b4 ♔f8** (there is nothing better) **2 ♖b6** and Black cannot defend both of his pawns.

b) **1 ♖a4 ♖a7 2 ♖da5 ♖da8** and now although Black has defended a6, he is helpless against **3 b4** followed by 4 b5 as his a-pawn is pinned.

27)

1 ♘xb3 is playable, but why move the knight out of the centre? So, we should take with a pawn. But which one? Remember the general rule, *capture towards the centre*. After 1 cxb3 White might be able to make use of the open c-file in the middlegame but he will have the usual endgame problem with his *doubled pawns*. Black will be able to use his extra pawn in the centre to make a passed pawn by playing ...e6 and ...d5. No matter how he advances them, White will never be able to force a passed pawn with his extra pawn on the queenside.

1 axb3 is most logical. It 'develops' the rook straight onto the a-file and it brings the a-pawn towards the centre where it will prevent Black from putting a piece upon c4.

28)

The first thing to realize is that the obvious 1...♖xd8 doesn't work. Instead of 2 cxd8♕+ ♔xd8, White has the *intermezzo* 2 ♗f6+!!.

The second thing to realize is that after **1...♖xc7 2 ♗xc7** the black knight is a remarkably good shepherd to the b-pawn. After **2...b2** the rook is blocked off on both lines: 3 ♖b8 ♘b4 and 3 ♖d1 ♘c1.

Always be on the lookout for ways of shutting defending pieces out from the promoting square.

The game was Krogius vs Aronin from the 1962 Soviet Championship, played at Erevan.

29)

Both sides have doubled isolated b-pawns, which could become targets later but don't matter too much at the moment. White has a passed, isolated d-pawn. It is rampant and well-protected, but is it going anywhere? Black has horribly weak dark squares around his king and f6 is almost inviting the white knight to invade. The problem is getting the knight to f6 with the black bishop attacking e4...

1 d7! deflects the bishop: **1...♗xd7** and the white knight invades after **2 ♖xa8 ♖xa8 3 ♘e4**. Now the threat of 4 ♘f6+ is decisive. As is often the case, the isolated d-pawn did not actually achieve anything itself – it was simply a distraction as it created the chance for White to do something elsewhere on the board.

This game was Emms vs Tukmakov from Copenhagen 1996.

7 More Endgame Knowledge

Earlier in the book you studied the basic ideas that you must know if you are to be successful in endgame play. You will have learned that endgames are usually far more complicated than they appear and that one slight slip can prove disastrous.

Now it is time to look into deeper endgame ideas. In days gone by, many players, even up to tournament standard, gave little attention in their study of the game to endgames. As Soviet Grandmaster Alexander Kotov once said, "If I get a difficult endgame I can wait until the adjournment and then look up the theory in a book or work it out for myself".

These days, matches and tournaments are scheduled to avoid adjournment sessions to prevent computer involvement. You won't get adjournment breaks! You have to know the theory. In many endgames, even though the position might seem simple, it is not easy to work it out at the board.

Endgames may appear dull, but dull is the player who does not learn the theory!

52 More About the Opposition

In '**16**' we saw that having *the opposition* enables us to drive the enemy king back so that we can advance our own king and promote a pawn.

We can use *the opposition* idea to drive the opponent's king away from the pawns he needs to defend. Look at this example, where it is Black to move.

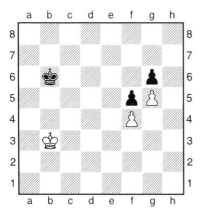

If Black is to win he must first capture the white pawns and then advance and promote his own.

But how can he possibly win the white pawns?

He will need to get his king to e4 to attack the f4-pawn.

But how?

Obviously he must advance his king towards the enemy pawns.

But where to?

1...♚c5 looks most sensible as it brings the black king nearer the e4-square.

But look what happens!

White plays 2 ♚c3 and gains *the opposition*. Black plays 2...♚d5 and White keeps *the opposition* with 3 ♚d3 (*D*).

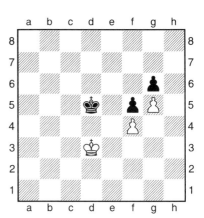

The black king cannot go to e4. In fact he cannot advance at all! It would all be different if it were White's move in this position. Then *Black* would have *the opposition*.

So in the original position Black must play **1...♚b5!** and after **2 ♚c3 ♚c5 3 ♚d3 ♚d5** we have the same position, only now it is White's turn to move. White must play **4 ♚e3** to keep the black king out of e4, but after **4...♚c4 5 ♚e2 ♚d4 6 ♚f3 ♚d3** (*D*) Black has gained *the side opposition* and White's king will be driven away from the f4-pawn.

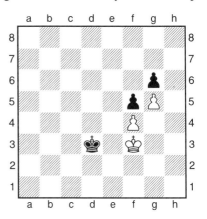

7 ♔f2 ♚e4 8 ♔g3 ♚e3 *(D)*

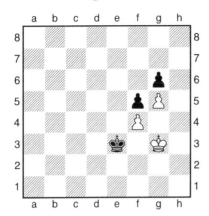

Black still has *the side opposition* and White can resign, since he cannot save his pawns.

In the next diagram White can use the same *side opposition* idea to win the black pawn – but will this be sufficient to win the game?

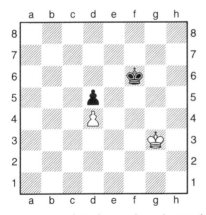

No! After **1 ♔f4 ♚e6 2 ♔g5 ♚e7 3 ♔f5 ♚d6 4 ♔f6** *the side opposition* wins the pawn for White: **4...♚c6 5 ♔e6.** However, Black saves himself with **5...♚c7!** because he gains *the opposition* after **6 ♔xd5 ♚d7** *(D).*

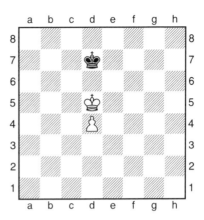

White cannot make progress; e.g., 7 ♔e5 ♚e7 8 d5 ♚d7 9 d6 ♚d8! 10 ♔e6 ♚e8 drawing.

It is easy to imagine that everything is simple in king and pawn endings.

It isn't! Be careful!

Try for Yourself 30

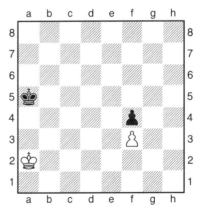

It is Black's move. Can he win the white pawn? And can he win the game?

(Solution on page 138.)

As having *the opposition* can be the difference between winning and drawing (or even winning and losing), you need to plan for it in advance.

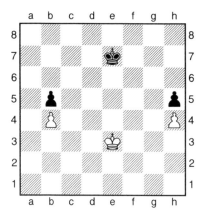

If it's Black's move in this position he is in big trouble because White has *the distant opposition*.

Black can't play 1...♚d7 because he will lose his h-pawn after 2 ♚f4.

Black can't play 1...♚f7 because he will lose his b-pawn after 2 ♚d4.

Nor can Black advance his king: **1...♚e6 2 ♚e4 ♚f6 3 ♚f4 ♚g6 4 ♚e5 ♚h7 5 ♚f5 ♚h6 6 ♚f6 ♚h7 7 ♚g5** *(D)*.

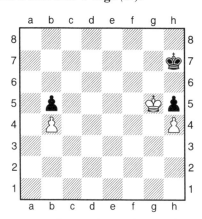

After **7...♚g7 8 ♚xh5 ♚h7 9 ♚g5 ♚g7 10 ♚f5** White abandons his h-pawn, rushes his king over to capture the black b-pawn and

then promotes his own b-pawn: **10...♚h6 11 ♚e5 ♚h5 12 ♚d5 ♚xh4 13 ♚c5 ♚g5 14 ♚xb5 ♚f6 15 ♚c6 ♚e7 16 ♚c7**, etc.

White is winning in the original diagram because he has *the distant opposition*. The two kings are a long way apart but they face each other on squares of the same colour. This means that however Black may try to close the gap, White's king can just step forward and oppose him. We have just seen 1...♚e6 2 ♚e4 but similarly 1...♚d6 2 ♚d4 and 1...♚f6 2 ♚f4 both give White *the opposition*.

Of course if it were White to play originally then Black would have *the distant opposition* and White would be unable to make progress; e.g., 1 ♚d4 ♚d6, etc.

Now that you know about *the distant opposition*, what move would you play for Black in this position?

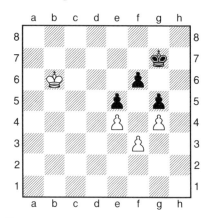

Score nought out of ten and go to the bottom of the class if you would have played the obvious **1...♚f7**. Ugh! You should have learned by now that nothing is simple playing around with *the opposition*! White replies with **2 ♚b7!!** gaining *the distant opposition* from the *side* and Black will find his king driven away from the f6-pawn; e.g.: **2...♚e7 3 ♚c7 ♚e6 4 ♚d8 ♚f7 5 ♚d7 ♚f8 6 ♚e6 ♚g7 7 ♚e7 ♚g6 8 ♚f8 ♚h7 9 ♚f7**, etc.

Amazingly, the only way for Black to save his f6-pawn is to play **1...♚h6!!** (D).

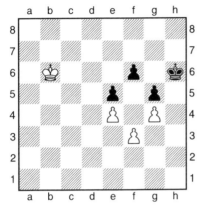

Now the two kings are on squares of the same colour on the same rank. It is White's move so it is Black who has *the distant opposition* and as long as he keeps it, White will never be able to win the f6-pawn; e.g., **2 ♚b7 ♚h7!** (keeping *the distant opposition*) **3 ♚c6 ♚g6 4 ♚d6 ♚h6!!** (D).

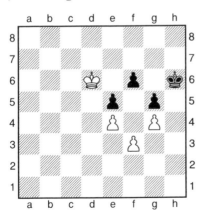

Brilliant! Black must be able to answer 5 ♚e6 with 5...♚g6 and 5 ♚e7 with 5...♚g7. He must keep the *side opposition* to save his f6-pawn.

Nine average players out of ten would play 1...♚f7 without thinking. That's why they will remain average players! *You* must give attention to detail.

Endgame positions may appear easy and rather boring, but they are not. They suddenly become very interesting when you find **1...♚h6!!**, save the game and show the world how clever you are!

At this point, I recommend that you go back to the start of '**52**' and play over all the variations again and analyse other variations in each position.

This may seem tedious, but the concepts are very important and will help you make the right decisions at the end of long games ... and after a while it becomes fun!

Try for Yourself 31

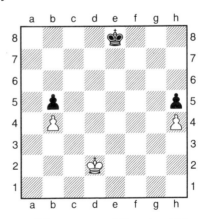

It's White to move. What should he play? (The solution is on page 138.)

53 Triangulation

It's White to move in the position below. Analyse the position yourself and see if you can work out who is winning.

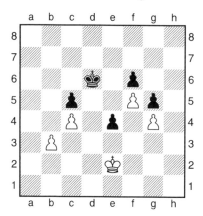

The first thing to notice is that if White plays the obvious 1 ♔e3 he has a big problem after 1...♔e5 *(D)*.

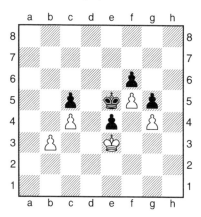

Black has *the opposition*. It doesn't matter that there is a pawn between the two kings; Black still has *the opposition*.

White cannot safely play 2 b4 so he must give way with his king. It doesn't matter where he goes, f2, e2 or d2, Black's king

will simply march forward and start mopping up the white pawns; e.g., 2 ♔e2 ♔f4 3 ♔f2 ♔xg4 *(D)* winning easily.

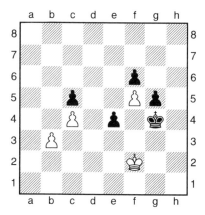

For White to avoid all of this and indeed win the game himself, he has to *triangulate* with his king.

White should play either **1 ♔f2** or **1 ♔d2**.

Black must then reply **1...♔e5** (if he tries 1...♔c6, White simply plays 2 ♔e3 and the e4-pawn cannot be defended).

Now White will play **2 ♔e3** and once again we have the position in the lower diagram of the previous column with the important difference that this time it is *Black* to move and White has *the opposition*.

The black king must give way and White will play **3 ♔xe4**.

In order to gain the opposition, White had to lose a move with his king. Instead of going straight from e2 to e3 the king had to move in a triangle from e2 to d2 to e3. *Triangulation*!

It's White to play in the next position as well.

Is he winning?

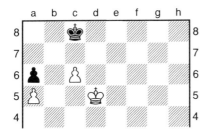

Let's look and see.

a) Let's try 1 ♔c5 ♚c7 (D).

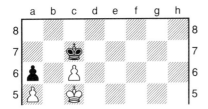

Again it would be great if it were Black to move. The black king would have to back off and White would play 2 ♔b6 and win the a6-pawn.

But it isn't Black's move!

b) So let's try 1 ♔d6 ♚d8 2 c7+ ♚c8 (D).

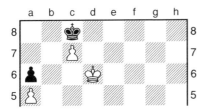

Now it would be great if it were Black to move. He would have to continue ...♚b7 and White would reply ♔d7 and promote his c-pawn.

But it isn't Black's move.

In both diagrams White is stuck because it is *his* turn to move.

White needs to lose a move so that when he reaches either of these positions it will be Black's turn to play.

White needs to *triangulate*!

In the original position at the start of this page, White should play **1 ♔d4**, when Black can try:

a) **1...♚c7**, when White *triangulates* with **2 ♔c5** giving us the middle diagram of the previous column, but this time Black will lose because it is his turn to move.

b) **1...♚d8**, when White continues *triangulating* with **2 ♔c4 ♚c8** (or 2...♚c7 3 ♔c5 winning again!) **3 ♔d5 ♚d8** (yes, yet again 3...♚c7 allows 4 ♔c5!) **4 ♔d6 ♚c8 5 c7** and we have the bottom diagram from the previous column and again Black will lose because he has to move.

Normally it is better if it is your turn to move, but strangely there are a few situations in which you are better off if it is not your turn to move!

In these circumstances you will need to look for a way to *lose a move*.

You may be able to do so by *triangulating* with your king.

54 Tempi

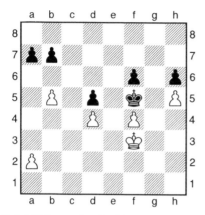

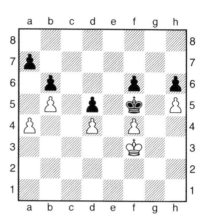

It is White to play in this position so Black has *the opposition*.

If White has to move his king, Black will win. The black king will march in on e4 or g4 and pick off the white pawns.

But what's the problem?

White doesn't have to move his king – yet. He has pawns on the queenside that he can move instead.

Yes, but eventually both sides will run out of queenside pawn moves.

And what will happen then?

Then it will depend upon whose turn it is to move. It will depend upon who has *the opposition* when neither side is able to move a pawn.

White has three possible pawn moves: 1 a4, 1 b6 or 1 a3. Let's look at them in turn to see if White can save himself.

a) **1 a4** is immediately disastrous because Black replies **1...b6** *(D)* and already White has no safe pawn move and has to move his king. Then, as we noted above, the black king will penetrate and capture White's pawns.

b) **1 b6** is no better. After **1...axb6 2 a4** Black gives back the pawn by **2...b5 3 axb5** and still has the last pawn move: **3...b6** *(D)* so White will have to move his king and again he will lose.

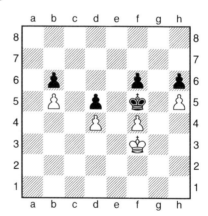

c) **1 a3** gives Black a choice. He can play 1...b6, 1...a5 or 1...a6:

c1) **1...b6? 2 a4** simply takes us to the upper diagram in this column, *but now* it is Black to move – and that is the key point!

By playing 1 a3 and 2 a4 instead of 1 a4 White lost a *tempo*; he lost a move, and against 1...b6 this meant that he gained *the opposition*. Now after **2...♔e6 3 ♔g4 ♔e7!** **4 ♔f5 ♔f7** neither player can make progress and the game is drawn.

c2) Now suppose Black answers 1 a3 by **1...a5** *(D)*. Can White still lose a *tempo*?

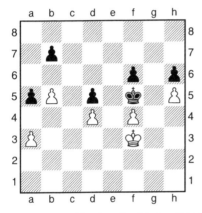

Sadly not! Following 2 a4 b6 or 2 b6 a4 it is still White to move. After 2 bxa6 bxa6 3 a4 a5, White has not managed to lose a *tempo* so he will have to give way with his king.

c3) If Black answers 1 a3 with **1...a6**, White has a choice between 2 bxa6, 2 a4 and 2 b6.

White will lose with both 2 bxa6 bxa6 3 a4 a5 and 2 a4 axb5 3 axb5 b6, but **2 b6 a5 3 a4** seems to work since Black has to give way with his king: **3...♔e6** *(D)*.

However, it is not so simple since after **4 ♔g4 f5+ 5 ♔f3 ♔d6 6 ♔e3 ♔c6 7 ♔d3 ♔xb6 8 ♔c3 ♔c6 9 ♔b3 b5 10 ♔a3 bxa4 11 ♔xa4 ♔b6 12 ♔a3 ♔b5 13 ♔b3 a4+ 14 ♔a3 ♔c4** Black's king gets among the white pawns with an easy win.

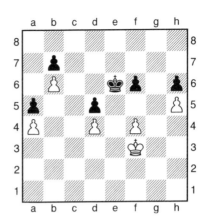

In all these variations, neither player was actually trying to do anything on the queenside. They were simply trying to arrange things so that when they had run out of pawn moves it would be their opponent who would have to move his king.

White was unable to save the game but you can see how careful you have to be when handling the pawns in such positions.

Try for Yourself 32

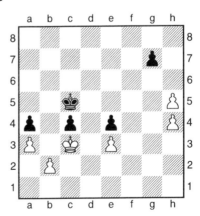

It's White's move. He'd like to play ♔d4 or ♔b4. How does he deal with the problem of the black king?

(The solution is on page 138.)

55 The Outside Passed Pawn

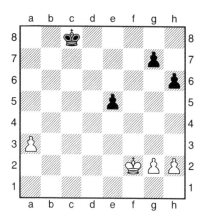

The material is level in this position but White is winning because he has an *outside passed pawn*.

White first attacks the black e5-pawn:

1 ♔e3 ♚d7 2 ♔e4 ♚d6

His next step is to advance his *outside passed pawn*:

3 a4 *(D)*

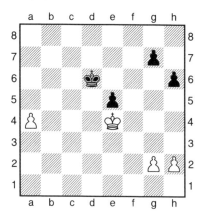

The a4-pawn is going to deflect the black king. Black can't allow the pawn to advance and promote so his king must go to the very edge of the board to catch it:

3...♚c5 4 ♔xe5 ♚b4 5 ♔e6 ♚xa4 6 ♔f7 *(D)*

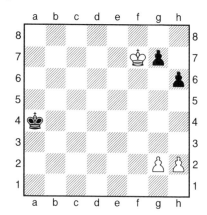

With the black king well out of harm's way, White's king is free to harvest all the black kingside pawns: **6...g5 7 ♔g6 ♚b4 8 ♔xh6 ♚c5 9 ♔xg5 ♚d5 10 h4** and Black's king is powerless to prevent the advance of White's pawns.

The same idea of *the outside passed pawn* luring the enemy king away from the scene of the action enables White to win in this position:

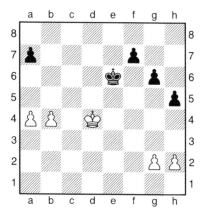

White doesn't have an *outside passed pawn* yet, but he soon will have! **1 b5 ♚d6 2 a5 f6** (or 2...♚c7 3 ♚e5 and Black loses all his kingside pawns!) **3 b6 axb6 4 axb6 ♚c6 5 b7!** *(D)*.

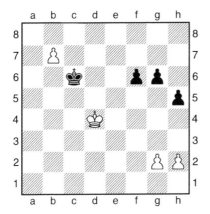

The *outside passed pawn* gallops forward. He has no hope of promoting; he is simply dragging the black king out of position. Now, **5...♚xb7 6 ♚d5 ♚c7 7 ♚e6 f5 8 h4 ♚c6 9 ♚f6 ♚d6 10 ♚xg6 ♚e5 11 ♚xh5 ♚f6 12 g3** *(D)*.

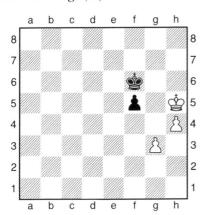

Black doesn't have a decent move! His king has returned to the scene far too late to be of any use to his kingside pawns. The variations 12...♚e6 13 ♚g6, 12...♚f7 13 ♚g5 and 12...f4 13 gxf4 ♚f5 14 ♚h6 are all winning easily for White.

If you were Black it wouldn't be much good exchanging pieces to arrive at the starting position in either of these examples and suddenly realize you were losing.

It would be too late!

You have to think about the pawn-structure throughout the whole game remembering that whilst isolated and doubled pawns may be weaknesses an *outside passed pawn* can be a big asset.

Try for Yourself 33

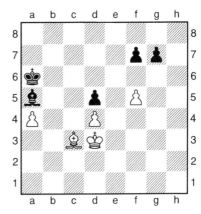

It is Black's move. He can exchange bishops by playing 1...♗xc3. Would this be a good idea?

(The answer is on page 138.)

56 Rooks Need Activity

The basic rule in rook and pawn endings is simple: keep your rook *active*!

In the following position, Black has just played 1...♖a7 attacking the a2-pawn. 2 ♖a1 is the obvious reply – but is it best?

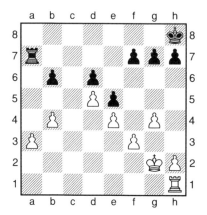

No! On a1 the white rook will be passively placed defending the pawn. Much better is **2 ♖c1** (threatening mate on c8) **2...g6 3 ♖c6 ♖xa3 4 ♖xd6** (D).

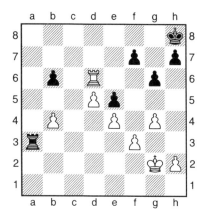

White's *active* rook now wins the b6-pawn and with it the game: **4...♖a6** (or 4...b5 5 ♖b6, etc.) **5 b5 ♖a2+ 6 ♔g3 ♖b2 7 ♖xb6**.

Rook *activity* is also the key to this position:

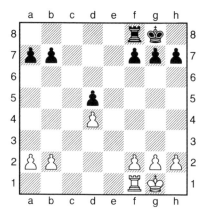

White immediately activates his rook and aims for the seventh rank with **1 ♖c1!** and Black replies with **1...♖e8**.

Both players spend a move avoiding mate on the back rank: **2 ♔f1 ♔f8** and White forces Black onto the defensive with **3 ♖c5** (D).

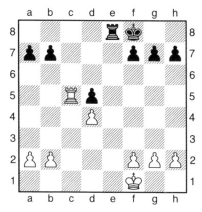

Black now has to grovel, first defending the d-pawn and then the b-pawn: **3...♖d8 4 ♖c7 ♖b8** (D).

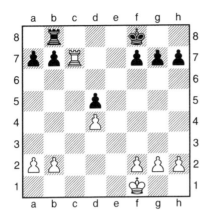

White could now play **5 ℤd7** and win the black d5-pawn but if he does so he will allow the black rook to become *active*: **5...♔e8 6 ℤxd5 ℤc8 7 ℤb5** (after 7 ℤc5 ℤxc5 8 dxc5 ♔d7 9 ♔e2 ♔c6 10 b4 ♔b5 11 a3 a5 Black is safe) **7...b6 8 ♔e2 ℤc2+ 9 ♔e3 ♔d7** *(D).*

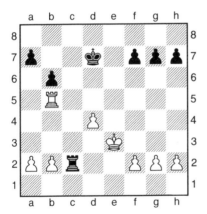

Black may be a pawn down but his rook and king are very much more *active* than White's, which are tied to defending the

b2- and f2-pawns. Black will play 10...♔c6 and begin annoying the rook. He should have no trouble saving the game. His *activity* is worth the pawn!

Activity is the keyword so **5 ♔e2! ♔e8 6 ♔d3** *(D)* is much better for White.

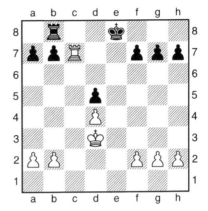

Now it is Black whose king and rook are tied to defending pawns and to make matters worse the white king is now defending the invasion squares e2 and c2 so Black has no chance of invading with his rook. Indeed, since 6...♔f8 is answered by 7 ℤd7 Black can't move either of his pieces! Black will just have to advance his pawns move after move, creating weaknesses and problems for himself as he does so!

You should always try to avoid allowing your pieces to become passive defenders and this especially applies to rooks in the endgame. The rook is very good at attacking enemy pawns, but it is much less effective when tied down to defence.

57 Rooks Belong Behind Passed Pawns

A rook will be more active if it is *behind* a passed pawn.

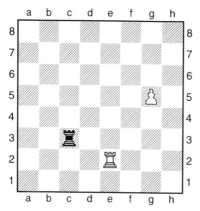

If it is Black's move in this position he will play 1...♖g3 to attack the pawn from *behind* and White will have to defend from the *side* with 2 ♖e5 (D).

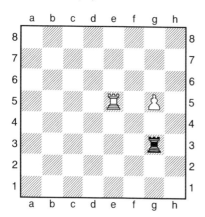

Now it will not be easy for White to advance his pawn any further.

If it is White's turn to move, he will play 1 ♖g2 putting the rook *behind* the pawn to support its advance and Black will have to defend with 1...♖c7 2 g6 ♖g7 (D).

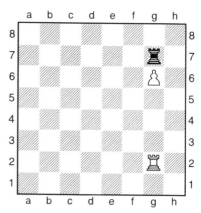

Now we can imagine a white king arriving on f6 and the pawn promoting.

If we reverse the position of the rooks, we see the problem of a rook *in front* of a passed pawn.

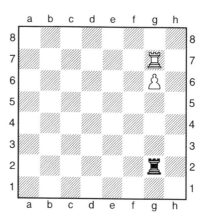

How does White get his rook out of the way of the pawn? With difficulty!

In the following position, Bobby Fischer was Black against Carlos Guimard at Buenos Aires in 1960. He had just played **1...e4**.

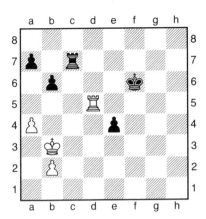

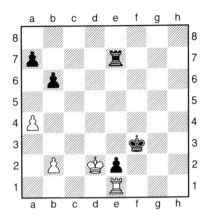

Play continued:

2 ♖h5 e3 3 ♖h3 ♖e7 *(D)*

Not 3...e2 4 ♖f3+ and 5 ♖e3 winning the pawn.

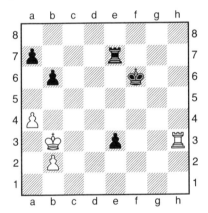

The black rook has taken up position *behind* the passed pawn. White's king will be slow arriving, so for now his rook must try to stop the pawn. The result is that the rook ends up sitting passively on e1.

4 ♖h1 e2 5 ♖e1 ♔f5 6 ♔c2 ♔f4 7 ♔d2 ♔f3 *(D)*

The ultimate position! The black rook supports its pawn from *behind* whilst the white rook can only wait to be evicted from e1.

Black threatens 8...♖d7+ 9 ♔c2 ♔f2 so White tried **8 ♖h1 ♖d7+ 9 ♔c2** and resigned after **9...♔g2**.

Try for Yourself 34

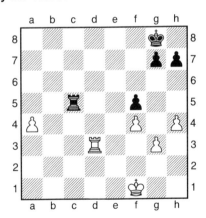

White has a passed pawn. How should Black deal with this problem?

(The solution is on page 138.)

58 The Rook and the a-Pawn

An endgame position which often arises sees one side battling to promote a passed a-pawn with the help of a rook.

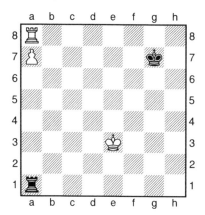

When the rook is in front of its pawn there are three important points to note:

a) If the white rook moves, the black rook can capture the pawn.

b) If the white king advances to b6 to defend his pawn and free his rook, he has nowhere to shelter. The black rook simply checks him and drives him away from the pawn by ...♖b1+ and after ♔c7 the rook returns to duty on the a-file with ...♖a1. White cannot free his rook.

c) The black king can only use the squares g7 and h7.

If 1...♔f6 (1...♔g6 and 1...♔h6 are met similarly) White replies with 2 ♖f8+ (*check!*) and then promotes his a-pawn.

If Black plays 1...♔f7, then White catches him in a skewer: 2 ♖h8! ♖xa7 3 ♖h7+ winning the black rook.

Now let's see how these points apply in some specific cases where both sides have a number of pawns on the kingside.

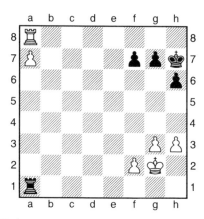

Points 'a' and 'b' still apply. White can make no progress with his a-pawn. Point 'c' doesn't apply because now Black can happily bring his king out to g6, where he is sheltered by his own pawns.

The game will be drawn.

In fact the game will always be drawn if the white rook is *in front* of the a-pawn unless Black's king is trapped on h7 and g7 and his pawns are horribly weak or White can create a passed f- or e-pawn to deflect the black king.

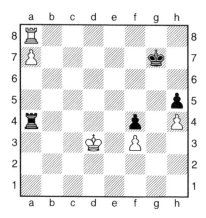

In this position White needs to get his king to g5. The game Walker vs Holland, Oxford 1962 continued **1 ♔c3 ♚h7 2 ♔b3 ♖a1 3 ♔c4 ♚g7 4 ♔d4 ♚h7 5 ♔e4 ♖a4+ 6 ♔f5 ♚g7 7 ♔g5** *(D)* and Black lost another pawn. The advantage of two pawns is enough to win.

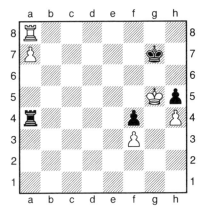

If the roles of the rooks are reversed and the white rook is where he ought to be, *behind* the passed pawn, White has a better chance of winning, especially if Black's kingside pawns are weak.

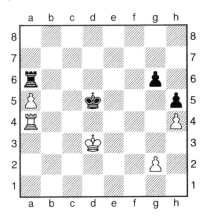

Now White has a plan. If his king gets to b5 he will drive Black's rook away.

So, **1 ♔c3 ♚c5 2 ♔b3 ♚b5 3 ♖a1** *(D)*.

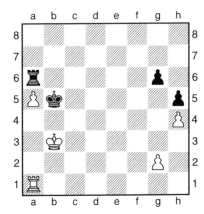

Black has prevented the white king from reaching b5 but he still has a problem.

He can't play 3...♖xa5 4 ♖xa5+ ♚xa5 5 ♔c4 ♚b6 6 ♔d5 since he loses both his kingside pawns. 3...♚c5 4 ♔a4, with 5 ♖c1+ and 6 ♔b5 to follow, is no improvement for Black.

So, **3...♖a7 4 a6 ♖a8 5 a7 ♚c5 6 ♔c3 ♚b5** (or 6...♚d5 7 ♔b4) **7 ♔d4 ♚c6 8 ♔e5** *(D)* and by switching the point of attack White wins the kingside pawns.

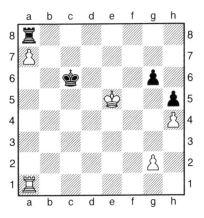

59 Cutting Off the King

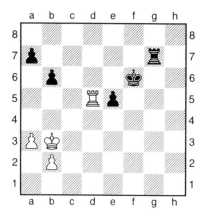

This position is from earlier in the Guimard vs Fischer ending given on page 133.

We might expect that Bobby should play 1...♖e7, putting his rook *behind* the pawn.

He didn't!

And why not?

Because after 2 ♔c3 e4 3 ♔d2 e3+ 4 ♔e2 *(D)* the king has blockaded the pawn.

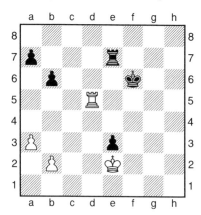

After 5 ♖d3 White will surround and capture the pawn!

Bobby's problem was the white king.

How to deal with the problem?

Cut off the king! Prevent the king from reaching the e-file.

Bobby played **1...♖c7** *(D)*.

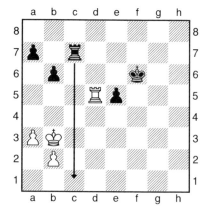

With White's king trapped on the queenside, only his rook can stop the black e-pawn.

OK, I hear you say, if rooks belong *behind* passed pawns, why doesn't White play 2 ♖d8 e4 3 ♖e8?

Good question!

Look back to the lower diagram in the previous column. Black had to advance his pawn without the support of his king.

Why?

Because on d5 the white rook is *cutting off* the king, preventing him from advancing into White's half of the board.

Now after 3 ♖e8 Black can play 3...♔f5 and his king shepherds the pawn to e1.

Kings are powerful pieces in the endgame. Rooks control lines.

Use your rooks to *cut off* your opponent's king from the action!

60 Zugzwang

Zugzwang is a chess term to describe a situation in which it is your turn to move and you wish it weren't! If you could just sit there and do nothing, if you could just pass, you would be OK ... but you can't, and any move you make leads to disaster.

If it is Black's move in the diagram below, he is in *zugzwang*.

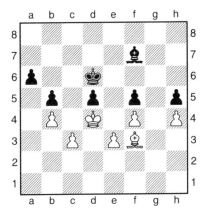

Black has ten legal moves and they all lose material!

He can't move his king. If he does, White will play ♔e5 or ♔c5 and start collecting pawns.

He can't move his bishop. If he does, White will play either ♗xd5 or ♗xh5.

He can't move his a-pawn. If he does, it will be captured.

If Black could leave all his pieces where they are, everything would be fine as White has no way of breaking into his position.

But he can't; he has to move something, so he is in *zugzwang*.

You have seen before when fighting to gain the opposition (which is a special type of zugzwang) that it is sometimes useful to be able to *lose* a move. And that is just the case here. White needs to manoeuvre and return to the diagrammed position with Black to play. Then Black will be in *zugzwang*.

How does White lose a move?

Can he triangulate with his king?

No. He must lose a move with his bishop. Here's how!

1 ♗e2 and now Black must move his bishop to a square where it still defends the h5-pawn. One possible continuation is: **1...♗e8 2 ♗d3 ♗g6 3 ♗c2 ♗h7 4 ♗b3 ♗g8**. The white bishop has an almost magnetic effect. Every move the black bishop has to follow him, defending the attacked pawns. **5 ♗d1 ♗f7 6 ♗f3** and we are back where we started, only White has managed to lose a move! It is now Black to play and he is in *zugzwang*.

Try for Yourself 35

Suppose instead of 1...♗e8 Black had played 1...♗g6 in the variation above. How would White have won then? Remember you are just manoeuvring your bishop around so that you will be ready to play ♗f3 as soon as Black has been forced to play ...♗f7.

(The solution is on page 138.)

61 Exchanging in the Endgame

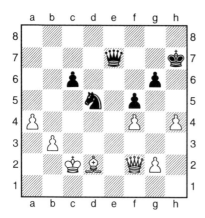

Here, White is two pawns ahead and he should win with his extra material. However, Black's queen and knight are strong and active. Winning won't be easy and it will certainly take a long time.

If White were able to exchange all the pieces, it would be easy:

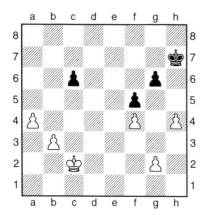

Winning the king and pawn ending is simple for White.

This gives you the first general rule: if you are winning on material, try to exchange *pieces*.

The second general rule is that if you are behind on material, the more *pawns* you can exchange, the better.

Pawns can become queens!

In the next example, from the game Epashin vs Galimov from Leningrad 1977, Black is a piece for a pawn down and looks in big trouble.

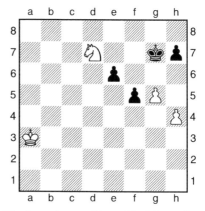

Black can't save himself with 1...♚g6 because of 2 ♘f8+ forking everything; e.g., 2...♚h5 3 ♘xh7 ♚xh4 4 g6 and the pawn queens.

However, Black can solve his problems if he manages to eliminate all the *pawns*. White cannot force mate with just king and knight.

One way to draw is 1...f4! 2 ♘e5 h6 3 g6 f3 4 ♘xf3 ♚xg6 and ...♚h5-g4. In the game he chose another way to achieve the same goal:

Black played **1...h6!**. If White exchanges pawns by 2 gxh6+ ♚xh6, he is left with just one pawn. This is the point of Black's play. If he can eliminate this last pawn, the game will be drawn. And that is just what will happen: 3 ♘e5 ♚h5 4 ♘f3 e5 *(D)*.

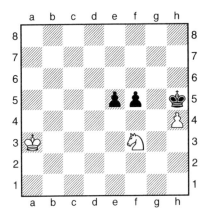

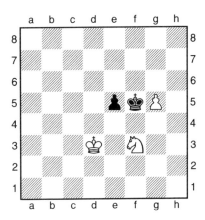

If White doesn't play 5 ②xe5, the pawn will advance to e4 and attack the knight.

Either way, the knight disappears from f3 and the h4-pawn drops.

In the game Epashin tried **2 ②e5 hxg5 3 hxg5** *(D)* and he seemed to be controlling h6, g6 and f6 very nicely. However...

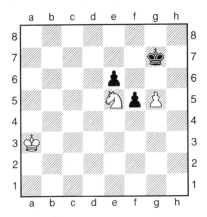

3...f4! 4 ⌷b3 f3!

Pawns don't matter to Black. He's not trying to win. All Black is interested in is destroying the g5-pawn!

5 ②xf3 ⌷g6 6 ⌷c3 e5 7 ⌷d3 ⌷f5 *(D)*

Here a draw was agreed. When the black pawn advances to e4, White's knight will be driven away from f3, after which the g5-pawn is lost.

If you are winning, exchange *pieces*: if you are losing, exchange *pawns*!

Try for Yourself 36

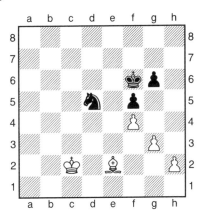

White has an extra pawn. What is the simplest way for Black to hold the draw?

(The solution is on page 138.)

Try for Yourself Solutions

30)

Yes and Yes! Black uses *the side opposition* idea to win the pawn: **1...♚a4 2 ♚b2 ♚b4 3 ♚c2 ♚c4 4 ♚d2 ♚d4 5 ♚e2 ♚c3 6 ♚f2 ♚d2 7 ♚f1 ♚e3 8 ♚g2 ♚e2** and the pawn drops. Now after **9 ♚g1 ♚xf3 10 ♚f1** even though White has the opposition he cannot prevent the pawn from promoting: **10...♚e3 11 ♚e1 f3 12 ♚f1 f2 13 ♚g2 ♚e2**, etc. Note that Black gets nowhere with the immediate 1...♚b4? 2 ♚b2 ♚c4 3 ♚c2 ♚d4 4 ♚d2, etc., because White has gained and kept the opposition.

31)

This could have been the position two moves before our first example on page 122. Let's try advancing the white king. 1 ♚e3 ♚e7 and Black has *the distant opposition*. 1 ♚d3 ♚d7 is just the same, as is 1 ♚c3 ♚e7! 2 ♚d4 ♚d6. To win, White must get *the distant opposition*. He does this by **1 ♚e2!**. Now 1...♚e7 2 ♚e3 gives the position in the example we saw in '**55**', which White is winning. 1...♚f7 2 ♚f3 and 1...♚d7 2 ♚d3 both lead to positions where White wins with *the distant opposition*. 1...♚d8 allows White to *triangulate* into the position he wants by 2 ♚f3 ♚e7 3 ♚e3, etc.

32)

If it were Black's move, it would be easy for White. However, it isn't, so White will have to find a way to lose a move and make it Black's turn to play. He can do this by **1 h6 gxh6** and now the harmless pawn move **2 h5** just wastes a move, leaving it Black's turn.

33)

Exchange! *Outside passed pawns* are killers when only kings are left on the board. After **1...♝xc3** (note that the immediate 1...g5 2 fxg6 fxg6 3 ♚b2 only leads to a draw) **2 ♚xc3 ♚a5** (the immediate 2...g5 also wins) **3 ♚b3 g5 4 fxg6 fxg6** White has the typical *outside passed pawn* problem. If he plays 5 ♚a3 to look after his own pawns Black will simply play 5...g5 and run his pawn home to g1. On the other hand, if White rushes over to capture the *outside passed pawn* he leaves his own pawns to their fate: **5 ♚c3 ♚xa4 6 ♚d2 ♚b3 7 ♚d3 g5 8 ♚d2 ♚c4 9 ♚e3 g4** (or 9...♚c3) **10 ♚f4 ♚xd4 11 ♚xg4 ♚e3**, etc.

34)

If Black plays 1...♖a5 or 1...♖c4, White puts his rook where he wants it, *behind* the a-pawn, with 2 ♖a3. However, Black can get in *behind* the pawn first: **1...♖c1+ 2 ♚e2 ♖a1**. This was how Smyslov was able to hold the draw against Lipnitsky at the 1952 Soviet Championship in Moscow.

35)

If 1...♝g6, 2 ♝d3 forces 2...♝h7 and now 3 ♝f1 leaves Black stuck. After both 3...♝g8 4 ♝e2 and 3...♝g6 4 ♝g2 he has to play the move he doesn't want to play, 4...♝f7. Then 5 ♝f3 leaves him in *zugzwang*.

36)

If you have noticed that White's bishop is the wrong colour for promoting the h-pawn, you are on your way! Black draws most easily by **1...♞xf4! 2 gxf4 g5!**. The white f-pawn will be exchanged and the h-pawn cannot promote.

8 At the Board

A computer has one big advantage over you. It's not human so it does not experience emotions.

It isn't aware of who it is playing and cannot be frightened by the strength of the opponent.

Its heart doesn't beat faster as the game gets exciting or as time-trouble approaches.

It doesn't become bored, irritated or impatient.

It doesn't have any fear of making the wrong move and losing.

It is not aware of any audience and it doesn't have friends or team-mates waiting to jump in and tell it where it went wrong and what it should have done.

It is not distracted by anything else in the room.

It is not concerned by the state of play in the match or tournament.

The computer can just sit there and churn out move after move in a totally unemotional state of mind.

For you, things are very different!

You have to learn to control your emotions and try to be a little more like the computer. Letting out a groan when you realize you have blundered will only tell your opponent he has a good move.

Getting over-excited as winning appears close makes it more likely you will make a mistake.

Getting bored or impatient with a position again is likely to lead you to mistakes.

Looking impassive, bored even, is often a good idea, particularly if you are setting a trap.

Looking confident is always a good idea, even when you are losing.

You should generally try to forget who you are playing. Play the board in front of you. If your opponent is much weaker, you should possibly try to avoid unnecessary complications and if he is stronger, you should perhaps seek complications as this makes blunders more likely and so randomizes the result.

In practical play there are three ideas for you to consider. Read on...

62 It's Winning that Matters

"It's not the winning ... it's the taking part that counts."

I don't know who originally penned this oft-quoted nonsense but he obviously wasn't a gladiator in the Roman arena! Nor did he ever exhaust six or seven hours of mental energy in one session at the board in a chess tournament.

It's winning that matters.

"The true value of a chess-player lies not only in his superiority as a sportsman but also in his creation of beautiful games that provide aesthetic pleasure."

I do know who wrote that. It was Eduard Gufeld, grandmaster and author. What he doesn't warn his reader is that in searching for beauty, a player may fail to prove his superiority.

It's the winning that matters and not so much how the win is achieved.

Kasparian unwittingly provided a good example:

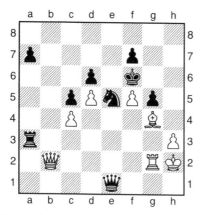

Kasparian (as Black) had outplayed Romanovsky in their game in the semi-final of the Soviet Championship of 1938.

Kasparian had an extra pawn, the better pawn-structure, a good knight against a bad bishop, the safer king and more actively placed pieces. He only had to play sensibly and patiently to convert his advantage into a win.

Genrikh Kasparian, however, was not just a master at the chessboard. He was a brilliant composer of chess studies and was to become an International Grandmaster for Chess Composition. He devoted much of his life to composing chess positions which had clever, artistic and unusual variations hidden within them.

When Kasparian reached this position his eyes lit up! He had found a study-like finish. He had seen **1...♖xh3+** *(D)* and realized that Romanovsky would have to capture the rook.

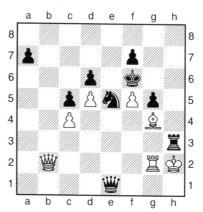

He had seen that 2 ♔xh3 ♕h4# was mate.
He had seen that 2 ♗xh3 ♘f3 was mate.
Wonderful! For a study composer this was an absolute delight. To beat the great Romanovsky, the first Soviet chess-player to be awarded his nation's highest honour, 'Master of Sport', was one thing. To outplay

him and crown the victory with a beautiful combination would be something else!

Kasparian gleefully played **1...♖xh3+** and Romanovsky replied **2 ♗xh3**. Kasparian's hand snaked out to grasp his knight but the smile left his face as Romanovsky's hand landed firmly on top of his. As realization dawned that his knight was *pinned*, Kasparian had to resign.

In his excitement and in his desire to be artistic and clever, Kasparian had thrown away several hours' work, victory over a famous name and qualification for the Soviet Championship. He had also been reminded that *winning matters*.

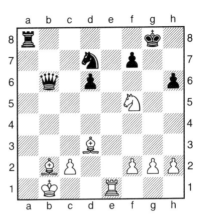

Black has gained f8 as an escape-square for his king and White has learned that *it is winning that matters*!

Lasker, Capablanca, Alekhine, Euwe, Botvinnik, Smyslov, Tal, Petrosian, Spassky, Fischer, Karpov, Kasparov, Kramnik. World Chess Champions!

And what are they famous for?

For being World Chess Champion.

Really only Mikhail Tal is remembered for his style of play and spectacular sacrificial games. The others all played (or still play) wonderful chess but they will be remembered more for *what* they achieved rather than *how* they did it.

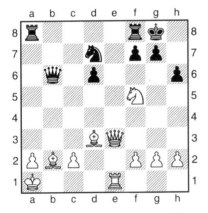

The junior who was White in this position saw that he could give checkmate by 1 ♘e7+ ♔h8 2 ♕xh6#.

However, he played **1 ♕xh6** and proudly looked around to ensure that there was an audience to notice 1...gxh6 2 ♘xh6# and admire the brilliance of his queen sacrifice.

Black simply played **1...♖xa2+ 2 ♔xa2 ♖a8+ 3 ♔b1 gxh6** (D) and won easily.

Remember: your aim at the chessboard is to *win*. You are not there to be clever. You are not there to be an artist. You are there to get one point next to your name on the scoresheet. If you can play a great game at the same time so much the better – but don't try to be too clever.

It is winning that matters.

63 The Art of Swindling

Mikhail Tal was losing. There was no doubt about it. He had played the opening dreadfully and by move 18 he had lost a rook.

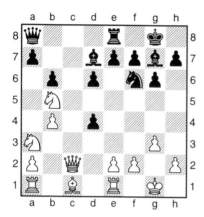

No doubt Tal gave serious consideration to resigning.

It is very easy to become demoralized and resign quickly after you have played badly or blundered away material. However, you should never resign until you are absolutely certain there is no hope left in the position.

So Tal looked to see if he had any hope at all. What do you think? Does he have any compensation for his rook?

Well, he has two extra pawns.

He has a lead in development.

He has an excellent pawn-structure.

His pieces coordinate well.

There are no weaknesses in his position.

His g7-bishop has hidden threats against White's a1-rook.

White's pieces have deserted their king.

There are weak light squares around the white king for him to attack.

Tal in fact has quite a lot of little things going for him. Added together, they certainly aren't worth a rook but they are at least something to work with.

That said, what Tal really needs is a little help from his opponent!

In this game from the Amsterdam Interzonal of 1964, Tal's opponent was the Hungarian grandmaster Lajos Portisch, a top player and a man not noted for his chessboard generosity. Portisch would need to be encouraged to make a mistake; he would have to be *swindled*.

The game continued **18...♖c8 19 ♕d1 ♘e4 20 f3 a6 21 ♘xd4 ♕d5** (D).

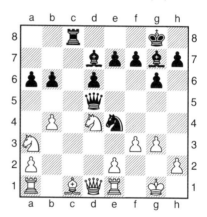

Your first step in trying to *swindle* your opponent is to give him plenty to think about. Tal is complicating things so that at every move Portisch has a lot of possibilities to consider. All of Tal's pieces are becoming active. There is a threat to the d4-knight, the a1-rook is hanging, a ...♘xg3 sacrifice is in the air, and the c3-square is awaiting invasion by a knight or rook. 22 fxe4? ♕xd4+ 23 ♕xd4 ♗xd4+ is great for Black so the game continued **22 ♗e3 ♖c3 23 ♘dc2 ♕f5 24 g4 ♕e6 25 ♗d4 h5 26 ♗xg7 hxg4** (D).

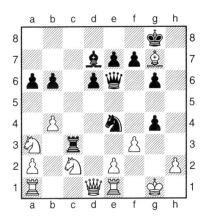

As Tal said, "He kept capturing my pieces, so I smashed up his king's position." Most of the time Tal is not playing the *'best' move* in the position. He is playing moves that make the game more and more complicated and give him the best practical chance of *swindling* Portisch. He is seeking moves that will put fear and doubt in Portisch's mind, and will lead him to make a mistake.

So for a moment just put yourself in Portisch's place. You've been winning for a long time but your opponent hasn't resigned. Instead he's been activating his pieces and complicating the position. It's frustrating; it's irritating. Tal is a rook and a knight down. His existing rook and knight are both *en prise*. Yet he still won't lie down and die! Now he is smashing up your king's position. You must still be winning but ...

27 ♘d4 ♕d5 28 fxe4 ♕xe4 29 ♘f3 ♕e3+ 30 ♔h1 ♗c6

... your frustration and irritation have passed through anxiety and worry and arrived on the doorstep of fear. Portisch

would have been trying to stay calm as he waded through the confusing complications in front of him but he would have been fearing the danger to his king, and he would undoubtedly have been wasting time thinking and cursing to himself about what might have been done earlier to have avoided this mess!

31 ♖f1?

In fact, if Portisch had been able to focus on the chess position before him, he might now have found an accurate move such as 31 ♘c2 or 31 ♕d4, when he should still be winning. Instead ...

31...♖xa3 32 ♕c1 gxf3 33 ♕xc6 ♕xe2 34 ♖g1 ♔xg7 35 ♖ae1 ♕d2 *(D)*

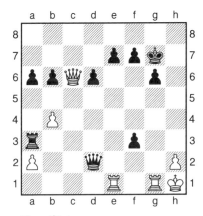

36 ♖d1 ♕e2

Tal, who might well have considered playing for a win with 36...♕xb4, settles for a draw by repetition.

37 ♖de1 ♕d2 ½-½

If you are losing, try to *swindle* your opponent by complicating the position as much as possible. Make him worry. Put in his mind the confusion, doubt and fear that will lead him to make a mistake.

64 Simplification

If you are losing, you should complicate the game. You should try to confuse your opponent.

But what if you are winning?

That's easy! You should do exactly the opposite.

Keep things nice and simple.

Avoid unnecessary complications.

Don't give your opponent any chance of counterplay.

Paul Keres provided a good example in his game with Goldenov at the Soviet Championship in Moscow in 1952.

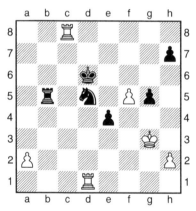

Keres (White) is winning. That is clear. He has the material advantage of a rook for a knight. But finishing the game may not be so simple. To begin with, all of Keres's own pawns are isolated. He wouldn't want to lose or exchange too many of them as he would be most unlikely to checkmate with two rooks against a rook and knight. Then there is the black e-pawn to consider. It is passed, advanced and dangerous. Then there is that black knight smack in the middle of the board.

As long as it is allowed to sit there, Keres will have to worry about the possibility of an annoying fork.

Winning could be a lengthy and difficult process!

Keres, however, saw a way of making things easy for himself. He *simplified* the position.

Keres played **1 ♖d8+ ♚e5 2 ♖8xd5+ ♖xd5 3 ♖xd5+ ♚xd5 4 a4** *(D)*.

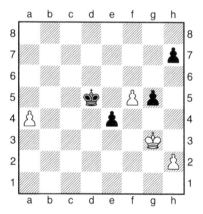

By giving up his material advantage, Keres has removed any possible danger to himself and *simplified* into an ending that he can win easily.

The a4- and f5-pawns are the key. Both threaten to advance and promote and the black king is torn between them.

If the king goes after one of the pawns, the other one romps home.

The game finished **4...h5 5 f6 h4+ 6 ♚g4 ♚e6 7 a5 e3 8 ♚f3 g4+ 9 ♚xe3**, and Black resigned.

Remember: when you are winning, choose the simplest route to victory!